BACK i

BACK in the USSR

The True Story of ROCK IN RUSSIA

ARTEMY TROITSKY

Faber and Faber   Boston and London

7 84 54

First published in the United States, 1988, by Faber and Faber, Inc., 50 Cross Street, Winchester, MA 01890. First published in Great Britain, 1987, by Omnibus Press (A Division of Book Sales Limited), 8/9 Frith Street, London W1V 5TZ.

Library of Congress Cataloging-in-Publication Data

Troitsky, A. (Artemy)
Back in the USSR.

1. Rock music—Soviet Union—History and criticism.
I. Title.
ML3497.T76   1988   784.5′4′00947   88-10956
ISBN 0-571-12997-8 (pbk.)

Published by arrangement with Omnibus Press (A Division of Book Sales Limited).

Cover and text design by Nancy Dutting.
Printed in the United States of America.

EDITOR'S NOTE

THE IDEA OF THIS BOOK first occurred to me after reading an article by Art Troitsky in *The Guardian* in the spring of 1986. When I subsequently learnt that Art was one of the organisers of the Moscow rock concert to benefit the victims of the Chernobyl disaster, I knew I had found the right man for a unique project. Much correspondence followed which culminated in meeting a representative of VAAP, the Soviet copyright agency, at the Frankfurt Book Fair later in the year. I am grateful to Alexander P. Runkov for his courtesy during that meeting, and to the following for their encouragement and assistance: Martin Walker, Andrew King, Peter Nasmyth and Chris Allen.

FOREWORD

ONE OF THE LUCKIEST THINGS that happened to me when I arrived in Moscow in 1984 to open a bureau for *The Guardian* was to meet Art Troitsky. I suppose it was inevitable. I had been asking around to find out who was the best person to tell me about Soviet rock music and to guide me through the cultural underground, and Art was the obvious man. If the far-flung and chronically disorganised Soviet rock culture has a single focus it is Art Troitsky. This is partly because of his rock journalism, which is outstanding in the Soviet press for its wit as well as its knowledge. And it is partly the fact that he knows all the musicians, formed groups with the rest and they all trust him to the point that when the Moscow Rock Lab was finally opened, Art was unanimously elected to the governing board as the representative of the musicians.

All around the country the tentacles of Art's connections spread. Down in the little republic of Georgia, tucked between the Black Sea and the Caucasus mountains, Art told me to seek out some friends of his called Blitz. It was like entering a time machine. Their entire act was The Beatles. The first half, they came out in Beatles jackets and Beatles hair cuts and did the early numbers. After the break, they came back dressed in the gear The Beatles wore on the cover of the 'Sergeant Pepper' album and did the psychedelic songs.

On the Baltic Coast, it was Art who took me round the bizarre, Bohemian sub-culture of the artists and experimental musicians of Riga, to the punk weddings and alternative fashion shows and the weird explorations of electronic sound that reminded me of the old UFO club in London in the sixties. In Tallin, it was Art's friendship that got me into the underground video-discos. In Leningrad, it was through Art that I got to know the wacky talents of Sergey Kuryokhin of Popular Mechanics who puts on performances with live goats and half-dead musicians.

In Moscow, whenever I went to one of the fringe theatres, it would have been Art organising the music. When Gorbachev's *glasnost* policies began to allow the abstract and conceptual artists to put on exhibitions, it was Art who would let me know about them and explain who was who and interpret the bizarre jokes that only made sense to a Soviet insider. He is uniquely placed to tell the history of Soviet rock, because so much of it would not have been made without him.

But this is more than just an isolated history of a small part of Soviet popular culture. This book is the first attempt by a Soviet writer to analyse the social revolution that has been slowly unfolding in the USSR since the end of World War Two. It is a description and an interpretation of a series of overlapping youth cultures, each of which presented its own challenge to the bewildered, surly and often cruel monolith of the Soviet Communist State.

This book can only be written now, and only legally published in the West now, because those successive social revolutions have at last produced a leadership in the Kremlin which is not tarred by the old evils of Stalinism, and which is well educated, reform-minded and not frightened of the future as represented by its own increasingly assertive young people. And with the men in the Kremlin giving their approval, the rest of the vast state machine slowly starts to move and learn to tolerate.

Human nature being what it is, we should not be surprised that the Soviet Union has been going through its own version of those social climactics that rock music has helped to catalyse in the West; the generation gap, the emergence of youth culture and youth market, rock as energy and defiance, rock as both symbol of herald and change. But this book is the first chance the West has known to comprehend the mechanics of this process from the inside, and from a Soviet point of view.

The fact that such a Soviet viewpoint can be so familiar and so easily understood in the West is a tribute to the global village. For decades, the Soviet government tried to seal off its people inside a cultural iron curtain. Western radio broadcasts were jammed. Western rock music was banned, and records were confiscated at the border. But the music and the message always seeped through. Borders have always been flimsy barriers against ideas, and these days they cannot stop the electronic spread of global culture. In Soviet Estonia, they can watch Finnish TV being beamed across the 60 miles of sea that separates the countries. In East Germany and Czechoslovakia, they can tune in to West German TV and tape record or video the music and send it back to the Soviet heartland.

The process had begun with radio and records. The coming of the tape recorder made it into an underground Soviet industry. Art and an entire generation of Soviet youth have grown up familiar with Western rock, and now a new generation is growing up familiar with video clips. The Soviet rock music that we are now starting to hear, and this book by Art Troitsky, is proof that the process works both ways across the frontiers, that they have as much to tell us as we have ever sent to them.

Martin Walker, *Guardian* correspondent, Moscow.
July 1987.
(Martin Walker is the author of *The Waking Giant*, published by Michael Joseph, 1986, and in paperback by Abacus, 1987.)

INTRODUCTION

THEY SAY ROCK is an international language, and William Burroughs suggested that language is a virus from outer space. Probably both statements are right. The bloody virus called rock music that recognises no borders has infected millions, made them shake and sweat and cry. At the recent plenum of the Soviet Writers Union some of our well-known literary figures compared rock music to AIDS, having in mind its allegedly demoralising and generally destructive effect on our youth. Yes . . . and the antidote has still not been found, although local experts have gone to great lengths experimenting with various drastic counter-measures. This is the chronicle of a curious epidemic that hit the USSR at least 30 years ago but continues to claim victims.

In some senses this book may be unique among rock books in that very, very few Western readers have ever seen the people or heard the music they will read about here. So it may all appear as pure fiction. (I once got a fanzine from the city of Gorky with information on dozens of local groups who had interesting names and intriguing ideas, but when I later visited the city I found that the entire publication was just a wishful fantasy of some bored disc jockeys.) Herein I've tried to impart a taste of reality, and not just list bands and dates and personnel changes and song titles. Practically all of what's written here is based on the personal experiences of those who made the history of Soviet rock. It's a book of personal confessions, mine and my friends', and I take responsibility for every line. This personal approach may make the final chapters read a bit like an autobiography, but in my life adventures I tried not to miss a single important event or interesting character, and since our rock life here is comparatively quiet and concentrated, this wasn't so unrealistic a goal. All my opinions are pretty subjective, of course, and I'm sure that some rock personalities here will be offended that I have given them and their bands less space than I gave to other, possibly lesser-known musicians. All I can say in my defence is that I've avoided the standard judgements and haven't followed any line promoted by the Ministry Of Culture or anyone else.

This book is not encyclopedic, and really not even analytical. Perhaps such more fundamental works will be written eventually, maybe even by me, but this is the very first book about Soviet rock—I mean really THE first, because there are no such books even here in Russia—and it is a rather simple one. I believe there are no exaggerations or embellishments, no special emphasis on the sensational or scandalous. I see it as a work of critical realism, at once strange and contradictory and traumatic, and my main hope is that it will awaken in some of you an interest in this unusual, undercover phenomenon—Soviet rock music . . . that you'll want to hear it, want to understand it, and that maybe you'll like it, as we like yours.

THANK YOU

Chris Charlesworth—for the initial idea and subsequent patience.

Dimitry Khachaturian (VAAP, the Soviet copyright agency)—for understanding and support.

Richard Spooner—for courageousness to translate all this.

Martin Walker (Moscow correspondent of *The Guardian*)—for all the above mentioned and much much more.

Alexander Ageev, Pete Anderson, Alexander Gradsky, Alexey Kozlov, Kolya Vasin—for information on subjects I didn't know much about.

Georgy Molitvin, Andrey Usov and many other photographers—for supplying my picture archive.

Alexander Lipnitsky—for just being a good friend over all these years.

Captain Beefheart, Can, Nick Cave, Joy Division, Lydia Lunch, Iggy Pop, Suicide, David Thomas and others—for helping me keep my faith in rock at various times.

Svetlana—for nearly destroying my work on the book when we met, plus help with the typing later.

Artemy Troitsky, Moscow, July 1987.

1.

*'You could give your soul for the rock'n'roll
The sound you heard from the X-ray shock
Of someone's broken bone
Once upon a time you was a beatnik, daddy.'*
—Viktor Tsoy, of Kino.

"I HAD BOOTS THAT WERE ABSOLUTE MAGIC; when I entered the dance hall, everyone stopped and stared at them. They were bright red leather—I don't know where our shoemaker found it—and stitched with fishing line that I bought in a store for hunters' supplies. The soles were crêpe, about four inches high in alternating dark and light layers. When I wore those boots I became noticeably taller . . . plus they were springy, so it seemed almost as if I were flying."

Alexey S. Kozlov, now aged 51, sits in his workroom surrounded by dark antique furniture, a Yamaha synthesiser and piles of video cassettes with tapes of 'Top Of The Pops'—the 'new model' Soviet composer. Kozlov is leader of the popular funk/new wave group Arsenal, but today I've come to discuss other matters. Alexey is a genuine surviving (and well-preserved) *stilyaga.** Stilyagi were a scandalous, outrageous youth cult of the 1950s—the first hipsters, the first devotees of exotic music, the first advocates of an alternative style. Kozlov's memory is undimmed by the passing of the years, his recollections vivid and deep.

*From the word for style ('stil'). The plural of stilyaga is stilyagi.

"That word—stilyagi—was not thought up by us. There was a satirical article in one of the central newspapers . . . They referred to us as 'mold' (a name that didn't catch on) and 'stilyagi'. So you see, it was intended as an insulting nickname, and we didn't like it at all. But the word style *was* key for us. We danced and dressed 'in style'.

"Dances were basically the centre of existence. At that time, in the early fifties, there were 'recommended' dances (the waltz, polka, quadrille) and 'not recommended' dances (the tango, foxtrot and others that we knew as the jitterbug and lindy). When an orchestra, on rare occasions, would strike up a foxtrot number, we jumped onto the dance floor and began shaking. We had three

13

dance styles; atomic, Canadian and triple Hamburg. As to where the particular movements for each one came from, I have no idea. Now, having looked at lots of films and music videos, I can say that they were similar to boogie woogie.

"The same thing with clothes—only much later, in 1971, did I first see a living prototype of our style. That was Duke Ellington, when his orchestra toured here. Narrow short pants, big shoes, long chequered jacket, white shirt and tie. Our ties were bright and long, down below the belt and wide at the bottom. My favourite tie had a silver spider web design; other stilyagi wore ties with palm trees, monkeys, even girls in bathing suits . . . I thought that was tasteless.

"We had almost nothing from abroad. Everything, including the ties, was home-made, and it was a real event each time a successful new outfit appeared.

"Finally, the haircut. The model, of course, was Tarzan—long hair combed straight back and smeared generously with briolin, sort of like in the film Grease. The back was turned up with a curling iron (I remember I constantly had burns on my neck), and definitely a straight parting. I even managed to make two partings, symmetrically spaced to the right and left, and combed up high in between. Of course it didn't stay up long, but the main thing was just to get it to Broadway in place to show your mates. Broadway was the stretch on the right side of Gorky Street between Pushkin Square and the Hotel Moskva where all the stilyagi gathered. There was a place there called the Cocktail Hall where we always sat on Saturday and Sunday. The Hall was open until five in the morning, something you won't find now.

"In wintertime our hangout was the Dynamo skating rink. We went there because they played jazz over the PA I even signed up for some kind of special lessons in order to have a pass for that rink. We would skate out in full regalia, in suit and tie just as we did for dances. And with nothing on our heads . . . it's amazing how healthy we were. We wore high-topped skates and skated all together, against the flow, slipping in and out among the couples in their heavy outfits and hats.

"Basically there were few of us stilyagi around, and almost no girls among us. It took special courage to become a 'stylish girl' —a chuvikha* as we called them. All schoolgirls then were brought up in a very strict spirit; they had identical braids wrapped up on top of their head like a halo and identical dark dresses with pinafores . . . whereas our chuvikhi had short hair (called a Hungarian cut), shoes with heels, checked skirts. And the suspicions people had about them ran much further. It was assumed that if a girl displayed such a free-and-easy manner in the way she dressed, then she didn't value her 'maiden's honour'.

*From restaurant musicians' slang. A male stilyaga was called chuvak.

"The reaction to us by the people around was always very strong, especially in the transport system, let's say, if one of us was riding along to Broadway. As soon as I entered the tram, everyone there would begin discussing and condemning me: 'Ooh, dressed up like a peacock!' or 'Young man, aren't you ashamed of yourself, walking around looking like a parakeet?' or 'Look, some kind of monkey!' I always stood red-faced. But it was even worse for the girls. I can only imagine the compliments they heard. They were lonely figures, literally. At dances we rarely danced with them; we danced with each other."

It's difficult to fathom the degree of isolation stilyagi felt living in small or even medium-sized towns. Which is why, in fact, there were none in such places. Besides Moscow, the 'mold' grew only in Leningrad and in a few cities whose recent history was 'Western': Tallin, Riga, Lvov.* But there was no association among the stilyagi of different cities, in fact not even the slightest contact existed. Thus the manner of dress differed from one city to another—the stilyagi of Riga, who made the seaside restaurant Lido their hangout, wore caps and jackets with zippers and padded shoulders instead of suits and ties. The passion for music and dancing, though, was shared by all stilyagi.

*These cities were not part of the USSR before World War II.

Technically speaking, stilyagi had no relation to rock; they listened to fairly old-fashioned jazz. Their musical idols were Louis Armstrong, Duke Ellington and above all Glenn Miller, whose 'Chatanooga Choo-Choo' was considered something of an anthem. The most important thing is this: the stilyagi were the first effort at a youth sub-culture, the first group of offbeat 'monkeys' and 'parakeets' striving to separate themselves from the grey, respectable world of ordinary 'grown-up' life.

Stilyagi were not only after kicks; one of their main traits was a hunger for information. But the Cold War and the 'Iron Curtain'* put an artificial and cruel limit on the exchange of cultural ideas. For a country as developed and urbanized as the USSR this was unnatural, if not plain outrageous. All the same, the Curtain did part now and then. Immediately after the war the country was flooded with American and other record albums brought back from countries where Soviet soldiers and officials were located. The movie theatres showed films with Glenn Miller and Count Basie (*Sun Valley Serenade* and *Stormy Weather* among others). All of this had a great impact. In the space of two years a whole generation managed to absorb these rhythms and their style . . . But then came Churchill's speech at Fulton, Missouri, and the atomic blackmail of Harry Truman. The Curtain closed again.

*Meaning the absence of contact with the West under Stalin.

Fashion and swing were not the only objects of the stilyagi's desire; the 'forbidden fruit' of the late forties and early fifties blossomed in abundance. During the famous and sorrowful 'struggle against cosmopolitanism' almost all modern artistic trends were declared manifestations of 'bourgeois decadence' and 'spiritual destitution'.

"We didn't spend our time just dancing to jazz. We read a lot —Hemingway, Oldington, Dos Passos; and we collected reproductions of the impressionists (we hadn't even heard of abstract painting then). All of this was 'not recommended' and therefore very hard to get."

"*I recall, Alexey, that in caricature drawings the stilyagi were always portrayed with long necks. Was this supposed to refer to their excessive curiosity?*"

"Yes, but also we had developed our own way of walking, with the head thrown back, held high and bouncing around as if we were constantly on the lookout. And there was a reason for the stuck-up nose and the arrogant gaze; we considered ourselves much better informed than everyone else. And incidentally, although we spent a lot of time in cafés and at all kinds of parties, we drank very little. We talked all the time; we found it more interesting to exchange new ideas than to get drunk."

Still one shouldn't idealise stilyagi and imagine that all of them were part of the 'intellectual' stratum to which the young Kozlov belonged. Many were really in it only for the weekend dances.

"I wore my stilyaga gear at all times, but other guys walked around like typical grey mice and changed their clothes only for Friday and Saturday. They turned into stilyagi for the dances."

There existed yet another, utterly unappealing group of stilyagi known as the 'golden youth'. These were children of influential officials, military officers, professors, etc. They were well-off and sensed their immunity from reproach, all of which led them into a certain lifestyle— drinking sprees in restaurants and expensive parties, often accompanied by fist fights, vandalism, even rape. It was just such an incident, when a girl threw herself out of the window of a high-rise building during an orgy, that served as the grounds for initiating a powerful anti-stilyagi campaign in the Soviet press. In essence, the 'golden youth' were not rebels, just examples of the seamy side of life among the cynical élite. (The social roots and way of life of the 'golden youth' of that time were examined in the famous novel *House On The Embankment* by Yuri Trifonov.)

"I didn't like what was going on with those people," says Kozlov, "but I couldn't refuse to associate with them since it was through them that I might find new record albums and magazines. The 'golden youth' had much easier access to information."

Stilyagi may have had differing backgrounds, but their look was uniformly provocative. And it was natural that a society so affirmative of its monolithic nature couldn't make peace with those who indulged themselves in the whim of looking so brazenly different. For stilyagi the hardest thing to take was the spontaneous reaction of their mortified fellow citizens on the street or in other public places. There was, however, an organised struggle against them as well, and moreover one in which no flexibility was shown. Unlike the tactics used in subsequent decades, no special attempt was made to figure out the causes and the essence of the movement, to somehow 'channel' or 'organise' the stilyagi. They were unconditionally considered to be morally depraved and a tumour on the social organism. The central accusations raised against them were lack of principles and ideals, and blind worship of the West.

My mother studied at that time at Moscow University in the history department.

"We despised stilyagi because it was felt that they were people without any spiritual interests, people for whom style or form was everything, and inside the form—emptiness. Dances as the meaning of life. And if anyone were to say this to them in so many words they usually answered: 'Yes, and what of it? What's wrong with that?' In our department, in our milieu, there were none, nor could there have been. They were enrolled mainly in the technical colleges, but often they were expelled even from there. I remember how amusing it always was to see them in the summer, walking about in their enormous shoes. It must have been very hot."

I don't know whether I ever saw a real live stilyaga. My first (and it seems only) childhood recollection of this phenomenon is connected with a satirical poster that portrayed a *chuvak* and his *chuvikha* dressed to kill in their stilyagi gear while a group of 'normal' people recoil from them in horror. The caption read: 'We Will Clean Our Streets Of Such "Stunning Couples"!' And it was not an empty threat; the stilyagi hangouts (Broadway, the Hexahedron dancehall in Gorky Park, the Aurora restaurant where Latsi Olakh's jazz band played) were periodically subjected to 'cleansing' raids. The main weapon in the struggle were pairs of scissors—pressing successive stilyagi up against the wall, the guardians of our strict style norms would cut off a healthy lock of hair (so that the victim would have to head immediately for a barbershop) and then from below cut the leg of his narrow trousers (no joke).

It's not hard to guess that the 'struggle' yielded no tangible results except to add fuel to the fire and prolong the inevitable passing away of the stilyagi and their scene. I speak of their passing away because a real death blow was coming, but from a completely different direction.

By the mid-late fifties the country's social climate had relaxed and the Iron Curtain had been raised. The information freeze, of which the stilyagi were a direct by-product, was thawing rapidly.

The breakthrough in the process of 'dis-isolation' was the Seventh International Festival Of Youth And Students, which staggered the capital in the summer of 1957. Thousands of real live young foreigners flooded into virginal Moscow. Among them were jazz musicians, beatnik poets, modern artists . . . even the political activists from abroad were fashionably dressed and knew how to dance to rock'n'roll!

Incidentally, the young Colombian journalist and future Nobel Prize winner for literature, Gabriel Garcia Marquez, was also there. I met him during his second visit to the USSR in 1979 and Marquez was amazed at the changes that had taken place during that time. He recalled that 22 years earlier Moscow hadn't created the impression of a modern city; it was slow-paced and lacklustre, more 'peasant' than urban. As it happens, many people believe that the breakdown of that old image traces back to the Festival, that after the Festival, Moscow could not remain the same. The stilyagi also could not remain the same.

"I had suspected as much earlier, but during the Festival we all became convinced that our style and our music and our idols all belonged to the distant past," recalls Kozlov. "Some stilyagi remained after the Festival, but these were the backward elements, pure imitators who were hopelessly behind the times."

The movement split into two groups: shtatniki* and beatnicki. The shtatniki, to whose ranks Kozlov gravitated, wore foreign-made zoot suits, baggy raincoats and short flat-top haircuts (Gerry Mulligan was the prototype). They listened to (and some already were playing) modern jazz—bebop and cool. The beatnicki wore jeans, sweaters and sneakers and danced to rock'n'roll. Kozlov:

*From the word for state (shtat) referring to the USA. The word shtatniki is still used, but as a name for Americans rather than those who dig American styles, music, etc. as given here.

"I had a jazz band then and we played some evenings at the architectural college where I studied. When we began playing things with some beat, rhythm'n' blues numbers, the beatnicki stepped out on the dance floor in couples and went into their rock'n'roll acrobatics, at which point everyone else stopped and began staring at them."

"Just like they once stared at your red boots?"

"Yeah, basically like that."

'Rock Around The Clock' and 'See You Later, Alligator' by Bill Haley became the first rock hits in the USSR. Elvis Presley was less popular and known mainly for ballads like 'Love Me Tender'. Paul Anka and Pat Boone enjoyed similar success.

All the crooners, though, were in the shadow of one Robertino Loretti—an Italian teenager who sang sentimental pop songs in a piercing falsetto. But Robertino's career was short-lived—the mutations of maturity affected his touching little voice, and millions of Soviet admirers mourned the passing of their first very own Western pop star.

The demand for pop and jazz recordings at the end of the fifties and beginning of the sixties was already enormous, while records and tape recorders were in catastrophically short supply. This led to the birth of a legendary phenomenon—the memorable records 'on ribs'. I myself saw several archive specimens.

These were actual X-ray plates—chest cavities, spinal cords, broken bones—rounded at the edges with scissors, with a small hole in the centre and grooves that were barely visible on the surface. Such an extravagant choice of raw material for these 'flexidiscs' is easily explained: X-ray plates were the cheapest and most readily available source of necessary plastic. People bought them by the hundreds from hospitals and clinics for kopeks,* after which grooves were cut with the help of special machines (made, they say, from old phonographs by skilled conspiratorial hands).

*pennies

The 'ribs' were marketed, naturally, under the table. The quality was awful, but the price was low—a rouble or rouble and a half.* Often these records held surprises for the buyer. Let's say, a few seconds of American rock'n'roll, then a mocking voice in Russian asking: "So, thought you'd take a listen to the latest sounds, eh?", followed by a few choice epithets addressed to fans of stylish rhythms, then silence.

*1 rouble = $2.00

Both the *shtatniki* and *beatnicki* were few in number and their heyday was brief. The imitative, decorative style and American mannerisms they cultivated were way out of place in the early sixties, when Soviet youth was full of euphoric enthusiasm over the flight of Yuri Gagarin, the Cuban revolution, and the programme proclaimed by Khruschev at the 22nd Party Congress wherein Communism would be achieved within the next two decades. Decadence and disaffection were completely out of style. The hero of those years was hardworking and cheerful, romantic and thirsting for knowledge, and, most of all, longing to be useful to society. In addition, he read Hemingway and knew how to dance the twist. So, some of the stilyagi's ways had become the norm, but there was something here that the stilyagi never had—a feeling of unity with the mainstream of life and a positive social role.

As for the ageing stilyagi still about, their reserve of alienation was so great that they ended up disaffected even in the new 'warmer' social climate and many turned to disreputable alternatives, becoming black marketeers, dealing in foreign currency and icons, while other 'idols of Broadway' drank themselves into oblivion. Only the 'intellectuals' among the stilyagi made use of their knowledge and inquisitive nature to become well-known musicians, designers and writers.

I have difficulty sorting out my feelings for the stilyagi. Yes, they cracked the ice of the Cold War with their wild shoes. Yes, they were the pariahs demanding their own kind of fun in an environment that sought to impose upon them its own prescribed ennui. And it seems to me that I would have been a stilyaga too, had I been born earlier. On the other hand, why is it that my parents, educated and open-minded people, were not stilyagi and speak of them sarcastically to this day? I can understand their point of view as well—they saw stilyagi as superficial consumerists who caught a glimpse of their 'style' through a crack in the Iron Curtain and added almost nothing of their own, save provincialism. The only creative output of the stilyagi was various funny rhymes and verses that they sang to the tune of 'St. Louis Blues' and 'Sentimental Journey':

> 'Moscow, Kaluga and Los Angelós
> Have united in one big kolkhoz.'*

*Collective farm

or

> 'Long ago the chuvakhi went underground,
> And there's jazz playing down there.'

This last couplet could have been etched in marble as a monument to an old stilyaga nicknamed Charlie, about whom Alexey Kozlov told the following story:

"Charlie was one of the main figures on Broadway, one of the leaders of the stilyagi. He wore a yellow overcoat and always had lots of records. I hadn't seen him for many years and then ran into him by accident fairly recently, about five or six years ago. He was standing on the same old spot, in front of the book store on Broadway, and dressed just as before. We recognised each other. He walked up to me, called me *chuvak* and proudly offered me a record. It was Glenn Miller."

Thanks, Charlie. What would we have done without you?

2.

'Plug the electric cables
Right into my heart.
Yeah, yeah, yeah.'
 —'Blue Eyed Demon' by Bravo.

THE BEGINNING OF SOVIET ROCK. Extensive research has convinced me that the first genuine rock group surfaced in Riga, the capital of Latvia. In a suburb of that Baltic port city I was met at the Imanta train platform by a man who drove a white 1937 Hansa sports car and took me off to his nearby country cottage. A gigantic 1940 Buick-8 stood in an adjoining shed. "My ultimate dream is to find a real rock'n'roll car, an American late-fifties chrome cruiser," he said.

The man is Pete Anderson (real name Peteris Andersons), born 1945, a modest fellow and 'eternal teenager' with large glasses and a flat-top haircut. He was never a professional musician, although he's been playing and singing rock'n'roll for more than 20 years.

"The very first group was The Revengers, although they didn't understand whom they were avenging or for what. Their leader and singer was a guy called Valery, who was nicknamed Saintsky. He carried an acoustic guitar with him everywhere and sang in parks and courtyards. His favourite number was 'When The Saints Go Marching In', hence the nickname. The Revengers began playing in 1961; electric guitars from Czechoslovakia were already in the stores, but the bass was home-made, using piano wires for strings. The wires were so hard that the bass player had to wrap his fingers in tape in order to play. (The first bass guitars appeared in the stores in 1967. A.T.) The group performed at school dances under a banner that read 'Go Revengers Go!' Their repertoire consisted of rock'n'roll standards by Elvis, Bill Haley and Little Richard plus black r'n'b numbers. For instance, The Revengers played 'Love Potion Number Nine' before The Searchers made it a pop hit.

"We got information mainly from the radio. I wasn't a member of The Revengers but we were friends and worked together. Saintsky didn't know English, and my task was to 'decode' the tapes he had and write out a reasonable facsimile of the songs' lyrics. When Valery was called up to serve in the army, I left home and spent a month learning to play the guitar so that I could sing and play in place of Saintsky. My first group of my own was called The Melody Makers. We had lots of influences, but leaned most toward black music. Wilson Pickett was a big hero of ours."

At about the same time, in 1963, the first Estonian rock'n'roll group appeared. It was called The Juniors and consisted of the three Kyrvits brothers. They later became The Optimists, and Pete Anderson played with them sometimes as guest guitarist. The *Pribaltika** machine started up earlier and began running on r'n'b fuel; in Russia things were a bit different. Rock'n'roll tapes were the ultimate new secret rage, but still not a guide to action; they did more to terminate the 'passive' stilyagi era than to start some new movement. We turn the floor over to Kolya Vasin (born 1945), a hefty, bearded good soul and patriarch of Leningrad rock fans. He's also creator and curator of the only rock music relics museum in the country, located in Vasin's own one-room communal flat.

*Collective name for the three republics on the Baltic Sea—Latvia, Lithuania and Estonia.

"It was as if some mysterious kind of romance, some supernatural poetry suddenly crash-landed into our humdrum lives. What did we have before that? Sterile, syrupy songs like 'Misha, Misha, Where's Your Smile?' or 'I Fell In Love With One, And I Don't Need Any Other' by bald-headed Eddy Rosner's dreadful orchestra. But I had a Jubilee record player upholstered in blue velvet and a friend who used to bring me records 'on ribs' in a shoebox. They cost 50 kopeks to a rouble each and I couldn't afford to buy them, but I listened to them like a drunk on a binge. Often we didn't know the names of the bands or the songs (the 'ribs' had no liner notes. A.T.) but we sang along all the same. I was hooked, and lost interest in everything else."

Alexander Gradsky (born 1949), the throaty Old Man of Moscow rock, lives near Leninsky Prospekt with his young wife and two children. He drives a big, broken-down, emerald coloured mid-seventies Buick (again!). He is now a recognised and entirely respectable performer, but remains a rather 'extravagant'* figure.

*Extravagant meaning unconventional in manners and appearance.

"I was in a privileged position—my uncle was a dancer in the Moiseyev folk ensemble and travelled abroad often. (Extremely rare then. A.T.) He brought me back real record albums. At the age of 12 I began imitating them, singing along with Presley and the others. When I was 13 I went to the studio on Gorky Street where they make audio 'letters' and recorded 'Tutti Frutti'. That tape is lying around here somewhere to this day. But rock'n'roll wasn't my only interest. I studied at music school, where we listened to Shaliapin and Caruso and Schubert and Bach. At home I sang along with Leonid Utesov and Klavdia Shulchenko* as well as with American hits. In short, I wanted to sing, but my head was in a muddle. And that's how things stayed until 1963, when I first heard The Beatles. I went into a state of shock, total hysteria. They put everything into focus. All the music I'd heard up to that time was just a prelude."

*Popular Soviet pop and jazz singers of the thirties and fifties.

Kolya Vasin also found meaning in life when he found The Beatles.

"A friend came to me and asked if I'd heard about the new sensation, The Beatles, and put on a tape recorded from a BBC broadcast. It was something heavenly. I felt blissful and invincible. All the depression and fear ingrained over the years disappeared. I understood that everything other than The Beatles had been oppression."

Gradsky: "Everything except the Beatles became pointless."
Alexy Kozlov (in a calmer tone): "Our rock music began with The Beatles."
To these voices one could add a chorus of millions. The Beatles' role in the genesis of Soviet rock is impossible to overestimate. I've asked myself why for years, and can offer a few theories. It seems to me that Elvis and rock'n'roll were nice, but too exotic for our public. The rough black rhythm, the fast tempo, the shouted vocals or hypersexual intonations were all magnificent and ideal for new dances, but how could we identify with them? They were as remote as America. The Beatles were closer, not just geographically but also spiritually. The Beatles had melodies, and for the Russian ear this is mandatory. Good rhythm and a strong, full sound are always welcome, but without beautiful, melodic lines the chances of success here are minimal. That's why The Rolling Stones were never rivals to The Beatles here, and The Who generated less interest than The Hollies or even The Tremeloes. (And why I sit right now up to my ears in letters from radio listeners incensed by critical remarks I made about Modern Talking in a recent broadcast.)

The Beatles' happy, harmonious vocal choir proved to be just the voice for which our confused generation was waiting, but was unable to create for itself. Liverpool delivered the solution. The well-known phrase "They must be Russians" would have suited The Beatles splendidly—as indicated by the phenomenal response to their music by our entire youth audience. I've often heard one and the same phrase from many different people; The Beatles hit the bullseye. Yes, they had everything, and if you want to feel what millions of lonely Russian hearts were lacking so terribly, just listen to 'She Loves You'. Joy, rhythm, beauty, spontaneity. Vasin the idealist uses one word to name it—'love'—that which can't be bought with money or won as a bonus for work done well or good grades in school.

The generation gap (here we call it "the problem of fathers and children") that was highlighted by the stilyagi and stimulated by the youth festival began to widen in response to The Beatles. The cherished and fostered 'commonality' of cultural identity suddenly started breaking up. Now it was not just an isolated gang of hipsters, but an enormous mass of the 'children' who said goodbye to arias and operettas, athletic marches, tearjerker romances and other formalistic popular music and surrendered to the power of alien electric rhythms. It was no longer just an expression of trendiness or snobbery—fans repaid The Beatles in kind for the sincerity they felt in their music. And the new language was so enticing and accessible that listening wasn't enough—people wanted to express something for themselves. Probably some wanted just to feel the happy enthusiasm, to imitate, to get high on the new music, but behind this stood something stronger, the "nationwide rise of rock", in the words of Kolya Vasin. Young people for the first time felt the right to their own, independent self-expression. Russian rock had lifted off.

Let's continue with Gradsky's monologue:

"Everything except The Beatles became pointless. I was living near Moscow University and often went to parties in the International Student Club. There were lots of student bands there, pop and jazz. Once I discovered a genuine beat group of Polish students. They were called The Cockroaches. I brazenly announced that I wanted to sing with them. At first they laughed, then they agreed. I sang the first concert without a microphone, and screamed so loud that one woman in the audience asked if I couldn't 'keep it down a bit, please.' I sang a few more times with The Cockroaches, then I met Mikhail Turkov. He was a typical representative of the 'golden youth' (grandson of Mikhail Sholokhov, Nobel prize winner for literature). He also played the electric guitar and sang. We found a rhythm section, Vyacheslav Dontsov and Viktor Degtyarev, and thus appeared my first group, The Slavs."

That was early 1965 and The Slavs were, apparently, the third Russian rock group in Moscow. The first was The Brothers, but they were short-lived. The second was The Hawks. The Slavs and The Hawks were rivals—Gradsky's group based its act on The Beatles, while The Hawks played songs by The Rolling Stones and, later, The Monkees. In Leningrad the first group was The Wanderers (early 1964), followed by Brothers Of The Forest, The Argonauts and Vanguard. All these groups played only at dances (in colleges, schools, student cafes and dormitories) and were paid 50–100 roubles per show by the organisers. All the equipment was do-it-yourself.

The Slavs' gear, for example, was put together by a certain Sasha Korolev and consisted of three 25-watt guitar combos plus a 100-watt PA. The whole set cost 1000 roubles. Gradsky recalls that the first rock concert in a hall with a stage and seats took place in 1966 in the Ministry Of Foreign Affairs (maybe because all the singing was in English?).

Gradually a rock community developed (although the word 'rock' was not in circulation—the new music was called 'big beat' or just 'beat'). The new social stratum differed little from those around them in external appearance and no special name for the phenomenon was used (except, occasionally, Beatlemania). The only distinguishing feature in evidence was that the kids tried to look like the Beatles—the familiar haircut, jackets with round collars and no lapels (called a *Beatlovka*) plus white shirt and tie.

Beat music fans migrated from dance floor to dance floor. There were, of course, no advertisements and all information about the shows was passed by word of mouth. The dances also gave rise to an extremely popular pastime—exchanging Beatles photos and memorabilia; swapping John for Paul, or a photo for a newspaper clipping about a Beatles press conference. Photos were even 'rented' so someone could enjoy them for a few days. Imperceptibly there developed an underground industry and a 'black market'—tape recordings of an LP cost three roubles, while the album itself would fetch 20 or 30 roubles.

The most devoted fans of Anglo-American music were the musicians themselves. Their sacred mission and chief concern was to sing and play as closely as possible to the original, to copy every sound and every voice exactly. And this was not in any way considered as unworthy. On the contrary, it was highly esteemed and corresponded fully with the audience's expectations. Tapes were still not very readily available and discotheques were non-existent; thus the beat groups compensated for the scarcity of sounds by performing as 'live jukeboxes'.

By 1966 there were already dozens of amateur beat groups in the major cities and the first festivals were happening. In Riga, The Melody Makers, Atlantic and Eolika played at the Dynamo sports palace. The latter group was known for its vocal section, and eyewitnesses attest that they played a Beach Boys repertoire (including 'Good Vibrations') that didn't miss a single note. The first Leningrad festival took place in a 200-seat cafe. Five groups played to a judging jury of *komsomol** activists. Beatlemania reigned—only Vanguard differed from the rest, with

*Young Communist League.

their singer Vyacheslav Mastiev, the 'Elvis of Leningrad'. He had a rich bluesy voice and sang everything from Bobby Darin to Spencer Davis.

The concerts and festivals ran on pure enthusiasm and individual initiative, and were financed by 'black market' selling of admission tickets (charging admission fees for amateur performances was a violation).

Fortunately there was no conflict with the law (just as there were no hair-cutting campaigns directed against beat fans). Society had become much more pluralistic compared with the days of harassing stilyagi. Total control was a thing of the past . . . replaced by total indifference.

It's strange, but true; the entire beat scene existed absolutely apart from any ties to official cultural life. Beat music wasn't even subjected to criticism as an oppositional, 'underground' trend—no articles in newspapers, no discussions at meetings. The various departments and administrations within the Ministry Of Culture displayed no interest and even the militia (police) stayed on the sidelines. During this period the cultural establishment was occupied with a different issue—the adaptation of jazz to Soviet conditions. Noisy jazz festivals were happening and yesterday's stilyagi energetically debated conservatives in the media, defending their right to their own chosen music.

Pete Anderson recalls how in April 1965 a Melody Makers concert scheduled to be held in the planetarium was cancelled, and an enormous crowd of fans stood for six hours outside the building, right in the centre of Riga, carrying banners that read 'Free The Guitars!' Some passers-by joined in the demonstration, but the militia stood by in bewilderment until the onset of nightfall finally dispersed the crowd. At which point Pete set off straight for Tallin, some 300 kilometres away, where he travelled every weekend just to watch a pop music broadcast on Finnish television.

It was only much later that I learned of the adventures of our first generation of underground rock outlaws. At the time I was 10 years old and living with my parents in fraternal Czechoslovakia (where they worked on the editorial staff of an international magazine). I spent only bits of my summer vacation in Moscow, and it was during such a stay that I got my first impressions of 'aboveground' Soviet pop. Incidentally, it wasn't so bad. In any case, there was a lot of lively music around. In the early sixties Soviet culture absorbed the twist. This 'soft' version of rock'n'roll not only gave birth to a mass youth dance craze, but also managed somehow not to upset our sometimes implacable leadership. The bureaucrats' attitude towards the twist was disdainfully condescending—as in, "Of course it's all nonsense, and the music is for idiots, but let them fool around, it's nothing terrible."

I remember a caricature in the satirical magazine *Crocodile*: a young couple in trendy outfits stand in front of a poster advertising a showing of *Oliver Twist*. The caption reads: "Let's go inside. We'll show them how to dance the twist!" Or a scene from the popular early-sixties film

Prisoner Of The Caucasus portraying a dance lesson—a comical, over-weight instructor throws two cigarette butts on the floor and begins grinding them synchronously with his shoes, whereupon he takes a towel in his hands and begins a motion as if drying his wet back. "That's the twist!"

Chubby Checker's 'Let's Twist Again' was the inspiration for a mass of locally-made twist product. 'The Best City On Earth' (about Moscow), 'Black Cat', 'Last Train', 'Hey Sailor, You've Been Sailing Too Long' and a hundred others. The pop idols of those years were Mooslim Magomaev, a handsome man from the Southern Republic of Azer-baijan, down on the Turkish border, with an ardent gaze and operatic voice, and Edita Piekha, a languid, purring pussycat of Polish ancestry who sang in Russian with a deliberately exaggerated accent. The stormy events of the years that followed caused everyone to forget the jolly era of Soviet twist, but in the mid-eighties there was a real revival of 'the black cat spirit'. Bravo, Standard, Mister Twister, Va-Bank and a few other young groups who felt remote from the heavy 'seriousness' of our rock unexpectedly brought back the pointed shoes, polka-dot dresses, stilyagi mannerisms and twist melodies. Funny, but it left the public at a loss. Was it a joke? A trick? A parody? "No, we just sing the songs of our fathers," asserted the leader of Bravo in a TV interview, and this answer, worthy of any good komsomol member, reassured one and all.

Now, listening to our old twist records (7" and 10" format, always 33 rpm), it seems to me that the songs are a lot more lively and amusing than the majority of Soviet 'underground' rock of the sixties and sev-enties. But I can also understand why the later rock audience rejected this product. It's not just the inane lyrics and the doll-like performers. The main thing lacking is a genuine electric sound. All the old re-cordings were made with traditional foxtrot arrangements, including horn sections and accordions and without so much as a hint of electric guitar.

In the meantime, despite obstruction by the press, the Liverpool charmers continued knocking at the doors of our hearts, while the local do-it-yourselfers in the beat scene, though operating in something of an informational vacuum, continued scoring points with the fans and corrupting them persistently on numerous dance floors.

A step toward official acceptance of rock music was inevitable, and at the end of 1966 the first professional beat group hit the stage. The first positive article about The Beatles, after a long series of sarcastic putdowns, was printed in 1968 in the magazine *Musical Life*, written by the jazz critic Leonid Pereverzev. Kolya Vasin recalls that he ran around Leningrad with the article in his hand shouting "We've won!" Of course it was premature to speak of final victory.

At this point we need to explain the fundamental difference between professional and all other musicians in the USSR, which it is important to know to understand the pop situation in our country. Amateurs (whose numbers may be unlimited) do not enjoy the right (formally, at least) to earn money from their performances, do not receive any material support from the official cultural agencies (at best they might be subsidised by some institute or factory), and in turn owe these agencies nothing. The idea is that they earn their living at their main, 'daytime' job or receive a student's stipend, while in the evening they're free to get into any activity they choose, even playing rock music. For professionals, music *is* their main job. They belong to an official concert organisation (of which there are around 200 throughout the country) and must give concerts on a regular basis to fulfil their financial plan. For each concert the musician receives up to 30 roubles, depending on his level of education, and professional seniority, regardless of the size of the audience. They can earn very good money, as much as 500 roubles a month, if they tour actively.

A professional group must present its show for evaluation by a so-called artistic council—a commission of cultural officials—who judge it in terms of commercial potential, the quality of the musicianship and the merits of the ideals reflected therein. If the show is not endorsed, it must be presented again, taking account of the comments and criticisms expressed. If a group simply doesn't please the artistic council at all, it can be expelled from the philharmonia (as the concert organisations are called) and in essence ceases to exist on an official level until it tries again to perform before some other artistic council.

Professionals have several advantages over amateurs: decent wages, the chance to tour, equipment provided free of charge, fewer problems with making recordings, appearances on radio and TV. Amateur status has one simple but significant plus: you can play what you want and however much you want. (This system changed somewhat only in the mid-eighties, when the first official rock clubs appeared, offering more opportunities to the amateur groups.)

And so, the first professional pop bands were The Singing Guitars (Leningrad) and The Jolly Kids (Moscow). The words 'rock' and 'beat' were unwelcome, and so these groups (and the dozens of others who flooded into the philharmonias) were officially christened VIA (the initials in Russian for vocal/instrumental ensemble). VIA was a disciplined (or, to be frank, a castrated) version of beat music. A VIA band usually had around 10 musicians in its line-up (rhythm section, two guitars, organ, some horns and a couple of singers, often with tambourines) and a repertoire including Shadows-style instrumental numbers, limp Russian-language covers of melodies from English and American hits and routine Russian pop tunes with soft electric sound. Dreadfully boring, but it was a stage in our cultural revolution and, in fact, a real sensation in the provinces, where people seriously thought that electric guitars were like regular acoustic ones except that you plugged them into the wall, like a radio, to make them louder!

3.

'Shut up mummy!
We're getting high.
It's psychedelia.'

—'The Chicken Farm' by Alexander Gradsky.

IN PRAGUE EVERYTHING WAS SIMPLE. There were several clubs in the centre of the city (Sunshine, F-Club, Olympic) and every week there were concerts by beat groups. The Matadors played like The Yardbirds, The Rebels played 'west coast', Framus-5 played r'n'b and The Olympics sang in Czech in Beatle style. My favourite band was The Primitives, the first psychedelic Czech group, who played numbers from the repertoire of The Doors, Blue Magoos and Mothers Of Invention. My favourite book at the time was, of course, *The Catcher In The Rye* and for want of a red hunter's cap I walked around Prague in a yellow chequered cotton cap with a long visor, eyeing all the stunning grown-up girls in mini-skirts, inhaling other people's tobacco smoke while standing in line for concert tickets, running 'Crystal Ship' through my head over and over again. I didn't manage to get a ticket to the first Czechoslovakian beat festival in November of 1967. Che Guevara was killed in Bolivia around that time, and several months later I returned from Prague with my family to Moscow, a city of which I had only hazy impressions.

The first thing I noticed in Moscow was the abundance of trendy bell-bottom pants. The first thing I heard, right at the train station, was a Russian version of The Tremeloes song 'Suddenly You Loved Me'. Life went on. A school mate in my new class took me to the Studio for Electronic Music, where Edward Artemiev and a host of egghead composers were experimenting with the first Soviet ANS synthesiser, which worked according to optical principles—you scratched any sort of design on a large sheet of smoked glass, and the drawing generated unreal sounds. The following summer, when the Americans landed on the moon, I got to my first Moscow rock concert, with the groups Trolls and Tin Soldiers. (Rumour has it that Tin Soldiers still exist somewhere to this day.) The concert took place at the Dobrynin beat club. New beat clubs appeared in Moscow almost every month, but were closed

29

down constantly by frightened officials. And in the late sixties there was indeed due cause for alarm; the city was shaking with a rock music epidemic. Hundreds of garage bands, thousands of guitars, hundreds of thousands of fervent fans. A real boom, the like of which hasn't been seen since; in scope, something like a natural disaster.

The list of bands in and around Moscow at that time, compiled by A. Gradsky back then when he was working on opening a new beat club, and preserved all these years, comprises 263 entries, including such remarkable ones as Hairy Glass, Little Red Demons, Singing Volumes, Soft Suede Corners, Russo-Turkish War, Witchcraft, Fugitives From Hell, Young Comanchees, Purple Catastrophe, Midnight Carousers, The Economists, Nasty Dogs, 1000 Audible Winds, Donkey's Tail, Cramps, Symbol Of Faith, Exploits Of Hercules, Glass Cactus, Bald Spot, Cosmonauts . . . one group was called Forgotten Pages, and that's just what became of the list and 95 percent of the groups on it. The rock fever had Moscow in its grip for just a few years, 1970–72, but that impulse kept Soviet rock going for another decade. And so, a look at those happy days. (Strange that there was no group with that name, though there were Winds Of Change and The Best Years.)

Fear had gone; the years of living in uniforms seemed like a bad dream. Soviet young people felt their independence, the right to their own values. But music alone and the exchanging of photographs was clearly not enough—something like an ideology or a new identity was needed.

Gradsky: "That something was hippieism."

Yes, the hippie thing refashioned our youth in the blinking of an eye. It seems to me that it was the most massive and visibly 'alternative' movement ever observed here. That is, even the numerous, noisy groupings of today look rather pale in comparison with the hippie phenomenon of the early seventies. I don't think that the philosophical, 'theoretical' side of Western hippieism had much meaning here; I knew almost no-one to whom the names Timothy Leary, John Sinclair or even Jerry Garcia meant anything. But the 'counterculture' lifestyle was taken up with enthusiasm by millions.

The hippie idea was new, but easy to understand—it allowed one to stand out from the 'normal' crowd and to identify with a certain 'progressive' scene. Kolya Vasin formulated this complicated issue quite simply. "The day after I first saw the cover of Abbey Road, I took off my shoes and went walking around Leningrad barefoot. That was my challenge, my attempt at self-expression."

The hippies' way of life and forms of communication were almost an exact copy of the stilyagi, only the scale was hundreds of times greater and different names for things appeared. Gorky street was no longer called 'Broadway', but just 'The Street'. And every evening The Street was jammed with long-haired kids and girls in mini and maxi-skirts, all decked out in beads and badges. The badges were home-made as a rule—you took a picture of your favourite group or a popular slogan (like 'Make Love Not War') written in English and glued it on to a regular, store bought badge. Once I saw such a badge with a portrait of the 19th century Russian writer Gogol (he had shoulder-length hair) and the signature of John Lennon!

Imported blue jeans were, of course, the preferred article of clothing, but local tailors were busy too. Lots of hippies made a living making trousers from canvas, sailor's suit fabric and so forth. The one mandatory attribute for all fashionable trousers was the incredible bell-bottom (30–40 centimetres across). The width of the bell-bottom indicated one's degree of radicalness and loyalty to the hippie idea. I recall that when I first met Igor Degtiaruk, the 'Jimi Hendrix of Moscow', leader of the group Second Wind and one of the pillars of hippieism, he looked at my tight jeans tucked into my boots with disdain and asked, "Are you in favour of war, or what?" He was dressed in some kind of pseudo-Indian home-made overalls with superwide flowered bell-bottoms made of curtain fabric, each leg embroidered in huge peace signs.

The favourite hangouts for hippies were in small squares in the centre of Moscow. The main hangout, near the old building of Moscow University on Marx Prospekt, was called the Hippodrome. However, unlike the stilyagi, hippies migrated a lot, especially in summertime. Hitchhiking became something of a professional pastime. During the warm months tens of thousands of longhairs gathered in the Crimea, making it something of a Soviet California. In Yalta there was a large market where hippies bought and sold clothing, records and all sorts of things, and earned enough money to get by on a bare minimum. The warm climate and the abundance of temporary 'communes' solved the problem of finding a roof over one's head. I once spent two months in the Crimea with just a few roubles in my pocket, filching food in cafeterias and at markets and sleeping in a different place every night.

Another popular spot was Tallin. There, between an ancient gothic castle and the Pegasus Cafe, was the legendary Hill, where hippies from all across the country congregated and where one could meet the most exotic figures—Buddhists with shaved heads, Hare Krishnas, other prophets and philosophers or just guys a little bit out of it after shooting up. Incidentally, drug use was not very widespread—the majority got high by drinking fortified wines. As to morality, free love was the chief tenet and was practised actively, often in collective form.

The authorities—specifically the militia, since the movement didn't come into contact with other branches of authority—were unsympathetic but tolerant of the hippies. The number of 'outlaws' was such that if an attempt had been made to detain everyone dressed in a provocative manner or engaged in amoral behaviour, there wouldn't have been enough militia stations to hold them. In certain especially uncongenial cities (Riga, for example) hippies were rounded up, taken in and forced to undress to undergo a test for venereal diseases. There were instances when lone hippies were taken in, and attempts were made to rearrange their brains with the help of fists. No such instance occurred to me personally.

Probably the most amusing aspect of the whole movement was the hippie slang, which was a mirror reflection of the language used by the heroes of A *Clockwork Orange*—Russian with a mass of slightly adapted English words, such as those for man, girl, old, new, 'square', crazy, face, flat, shoes, fiver, tenner and so forth, including the most popular four-letter words.

Basically, it seems to me that our hippies were a lot like hippies in the West, only more passive in society—tendencies like yippie and other New Left variations were absent here for all practical purposes. Hippieism was an alternative way to get alternative pleasure. And at the heart of it all was music, primarily Anglo-American rock. From this flowed the fashion, the slang and the endless hours grooving around the stereo.

Western LPs were the number one fetish. In the stores, of course, there was no hint of them; they were brought into the country by sailors, athletes, diplomats and foreigners, and the black market demand for them was high. A brand new record by a popular group could cost 60–70 roubles, while albums so worn out you could hardly listen to them would go for 30. If an album had a photo on the dust sleeve, the photo might be cut out and hung on the wall like a poster, while the remains of the dust sleeve would be glued together and the album would be sold for a bit less than the normal going price. Real rock posters cost 10–25 roubles, depending on size and content. Double albums were sometimes split up and sold separately. Old records were wrapped in Cellophane and pawned off on the inexperienced as the real thing. Barbarity, questionable commerce and fanatical love for rock merged into one at the market place.

In 1972 my old friend Sasha Kostenko (from Prague days) and I began operating the first discotheque in Moscow (at least I didn't know of any others). For 15 roubles we rented a PA from musicians we knew and transported it to a cafe at Moscow University, where we would spin discs all evening. We were paid 40 roubles for our efforts, which barely covered our expenses (if you include the wine we drank at the control board). The discotheque was atypical by international standards. The first hour was dedicated to listening; that is, I played music by 'serious' groups like Jethro Tull, Pink Floyd, King Crimson and talked about their histories. (By the way, that's how my mission as rock critic began. One evening some people from a monthly youth magazine visited the discotheque, listened to my 'lecture' and proposed that I write articles for them. The first, on Deep Purple, appeared in early 1975.) After the 'listening' hour, people spent the next three expressing themselves on the dance floor. A few years later there were dozens of discotheques in Moscow, and in some of them there was no dancing at all—people just listened and learned . . . which was understandable, since the press waged a campaign of silence against rock music and the public had to get by mainly on rumours. One such rumour is alive to this day, namely that The Beatles played in the Soviet Union at the airport in Moscow during a stopover on their way home from Japan, and that this incident was the inspiration for their song 'Back In The USSR'.

After The Beatles broke up, hard rock bands like Led Zeppelin, Deep Purple, Black Sabbath, Uriah Heep and Grand Funk were the provisional favourites among Soviet rock fans. The female minority and those drawn to softer music preferred Carlos Santana, Cat Stevens and Elton John. The more enlightened crowd was digging Pink Floyd, King Crimson and Yes.

In the early seventies rock was discovered by part of the respectable public, the so-called creative intelligentsia. The rock opera 'Jesus Christ Superstar' was a great revelation for them. They couldn't handle rock's bastard beat until they heard it covered with a veneer of symphonic instrumentation and packaged in pompous arias and overtures. To be honest, the rockers themselves were genuinely overjoyed. They loved their music, but had somehow succumbed to the idea that it was outside the realm of 'real art', and deep in their hearts felt not only like outlaws, but even a little like 'moral defects'. In the USSR the prestige of classical music is ingrained at every turn, starting in childhood, and thus from even the most fanatic rock loyalists one might hear confessions to the effect that "Of course Bach and Beethoven, that's lofty stuff and super . . . it's sad that for some reason I don't like that music . . ." Accordingly, it became popular to defend lowly rock by citing records like 'Pictures At An Exhibition' by ELP and 'operas' like 'Jesus Christ Superstar' and arguing that rock could prepare young people to appreciate the great classical heritage.

Gradually rock began to change from an isolated 'ghetto' into something more prestigious. The first musician in Moscow who sensed this and found the courage to take a step from the comparatively safe world of jazz towards the rock reservation was Alexey Kozlov. At the end of 1972 he joined forces with a group of underground rockers and formed Arsenal, a group complete with brass section, several singers and a repertoire of songs from Blood Sweat & Tears, Chicago and almost the entire 'Jesus Christ Superstar'. Kozlov introduced the idea of 'cultured' rock to the sizeable intellectual audience. Arsenal's first concert, not surprisingly, took place in Moscow's experimental Taganka theatre. One of the group's vocalists was an Iranian and, unlike the majority of singers, he sang in English with good pronunciation.

It was at one of Arsenal's early concerts (in a hall at the Oncological Centre, as I recall now) that I first found myself in a real squeeze in front of the entrance with the possibility of breaking some ribs. The heavy atmosphere was part of almost all the rock concerts at that time—the halls were small, tickets were few and the crowd was in a stop-at-nothing frame of mind, breaking down doors and climbing in windows. From the reminiscences of A. Gradsky:

"It was the summer of 1971. We were scheduled to play a dance in the foyer of the Institute of the National Economy. Around 1,500 tickets were sold, but someone had printed up another 1,000 counterfeits. My drummer left his sticks at home, and I went to get them, but when I returned the crowd around the entrance was packed so tight that I couldn't get close to the doors. I said, 'I'm Gradsky; I need to get through,' but everyone around just laughed and said, 'We're all Gradskys, we all need to get through.' (What a paradox—since the press and TV gave the rock scene zero publicity, few of the fans knew what their heroes looked like! A.T.)

"Still, we had to play the show, because we'd been paid in advance. So I had no choice but to climb up the wall, clinging to the water pipes and shingles. I got to the first open window on the second floor, climbed in and found myself in the middle of a meeting of the institute's komsomol committee. The members were stunned, of course. Well, I brushed myself off, said 'Excuse me, we have a dance here', and made for the door.

"The dance was lively, too—eight or 10 girls in the middle of the floor undressed and began dancing and waving their bras. The security people from the institute noticed this from the balcony and set off towards the scene of the crime, but by the time they got through the crowd, everyone had managed to get dressed again."

I don't know who those particular girls were, but we did have groupies here, and don't believe that they appeared just in imitation of the West. They went to all the 'sessions' (another popular English word that was co-opted and used universally to mean any rock concert), wore the most daring mini-skirts and transparent lace blouses, danced next to the stage and attracted lots of attention. They had no special name (the word 'groupies' never made it over here) but everyone knew who they were and treated them with respect. The ringleader of Moscow's groupies was a brunette of medium height with long hair parted in the middle and a rather seedy looking complexion (maybe just too much make-up). Rumour had it she was a colonel's daughter.

Things were certainly lively in those days—energy, enthusiasm, a new life, independence. Now it's customary to think back on those days with nostalgia, as one might recall a first love. To be honest, the atmosphere in general was much more interesting than the bands in particular. Almost all of them played the same things that had already been played much better on records. The 'sessions' were a show-case for all our half-baked Hendrixes and Claptons, Jim Morrisons and Robert Plants. They copied shamelessly, often without understanding what they were singing about.

But the audience wanted nothing else. Kolya Vasin recalls that The Nomads, the first Leningrad group to begin singing in Russian, were often booed off the stage and earned no respect. The Russian language was considered somehow an attribute of conformity, the symbol of some 'hostile', non-rock system of values.

The first hit rock song in Moscow sung in the native tongue was by The Hawks, called 'The Sun Above Us'. This was in 1966; before that The Hawks had played an exclusively Rolling Stones repertoire.

A bit later Gradsky composed his first opus, 'Blue Forest', while sitting in a trolley, and subsequently put together a mini rock opera with his new band The Jesters. The lyrics were straight from a well-known nursery rhyme but the on-stage presentation gave the piece a sexually suggestive meaning. On this basis he claims that he was the first Soviet punk, but in fact the first Russian-language rock songs differed little in lyrical content from the standard songs of the day. Somehow the songwriters didn't turn to their own images and problems for material (Bob Dylan wasn't too highly regarded here at that time) and that may be another reason for the public's negative reaction to such songs.

Finally, however, there appeared a band that sang something original—Time Machine. If there's any group on whom we might bestow the honorary title of Russian Beatles in terms of their influence on rock music here, it's probably Time Machine. Andrei Makarevich, the only son of a well-known architect, took one listen to an album his father had brought from abroad ('A Hard Day's Night') and, following in the esteemed footsteps of others before him, immediately effected a radical change in his views on life.

In 1968 he organised a beat group with his classmates from the eighth grade (meaning they were around 15 years old). This was a normal phenomenon; at that time there was a beat group in almost every school, sometimes several. I also had a little experience of the same sort. One of Andrei's band members, Sergei Kavagoa, had relatives in Japan and through them he became the proud owner of an Aceton electric organ (which was promptly stolen and then found by the Militia 10 years later in Siberia). For some reason, the young Makarevich was the only one who understood the Beatles' message correctly: "I saw that they were normal, completely natural people, the same as we were, and that they were singing about their own problems in their own words. I thought, why can't we do the same? Why do we have to pretend to be something we're not, from California or Liverpool?"

Time Machine's first songs were juvenile satire, full of the harsh irony one expects of school kids from well-to-do families. The most popular was an anti-consumerist number with the line, 'I'll buy myself a gold toilet', which was a bold and even rather serious lyric for that time.* Unfortunately, Time Machine played very poorly and thus didn't go over well in comparison with more established, more dynamic groups who had their copy-cat licks down pat. All this drove Makarevich into a quiet desperation that led to his quitting the guitar several times, but friends stopped him in time and a good thing too, for we could have lost our first rock bard.

A similar process, the appearance of native-language bands, was going on in other Soviet rock centres. In Latvia it was the band Double Ladybug headed by Imant Kalninsh (who later gained fame as a symphony composer). In Leningrad it was Saint Petersburg, led by Vladimir Rekshan (who exerted a fundamental influence on the present-day popular band Aquarium). All the same, these groups were a tiny minority compared to the groups still covering Anglo-American rock songs. Many people even felt that singing in Russian was just some kind of gimmick for those who didn't know how to play rock the 'right' way. There also existed the fairly logical theory that singing rock in Russian was practically impossible, in that the longer Russian words simply didn't fit into the rhythm . . . the future would show that the theory didn't fit in all cases.

During this same period the first inter-city festivals took place. An Armenian named Rafik Mkartchan with a well-developed business sense signed contracts with bands from Moscow, Leningrad and Pribaltika and brought them to Yerevan, where they played in a 6000-seat sports palace. According to Gradsky, you couldn't hear a thing because the crowd began screaming at the sound of the first chord, while the PA was only 200 watts. Such concerts were discontinued in 1970, when poor Rafik was sent to jail for financial machinations.

The only legal rock event of those years was a festival called Silver Strings organised in Gorky in 1971 by the local komsomol. Gradsky & The Jesters played 'Georgia On My Mind' along with a bevy of Iron Butterfly tunes plus two songs in Russian and shared first place honours with a band called Ariel from Chelyabinsk whose set consisted of electrified adaptions of old Russian folk songs. This little innovation became highly fashionable and was warmly welcomed by the cultural authorities, since it was felt to represent a sort of compromise between East and West . . . as in, OK, never mind the damned guitars; the main thing is that the songs are ours, our folk songs, and not some bourgeois obscenities.

*Serious because it makes ironic commentary on a statement made by Lenin before the revolution that under communism, public toilets could be made of gold.

The leading Soviet VIA band was The Songsters—a dozen young mustachioed lads whose high-pitched voices and block flute/electric organ arrangements were deadly beyond belief. Their records sold by the millions (maybe because there were no others around). In the mid-seventies The Songsters first presented the new Soviet pop music in the USA, but no one cares to recall that tour.

For all practical purposes, our rock music scene had no real international contacts. There exists an amusing legend (for whose authenticity I can't vouch) to the effect that the then-Minister Of Culture Madame Furtseva sent a special emissary to a Rolling Stones concert in Warsaw. He returned speechless, thoroughly outraged by what he had seen and heard, and so a firm decision was made not to allow the infection to spread to us. On rare occasions a beat group from one of the socialist countries would tour here, and each such occasion was a real event. It was strange and touching to hear rock music in the big concert halls. Kolya Vasin recalls a tour by the Polish group Skaldowie:

"I was president at that time of the pop federation,* whose main activity consisted of organising after-hours concerts in restaurants. So we visited the Poles in their hotel after a show and proposed that they play for us, at night. They refused. At that point I made a speech about how the beat clubs in Poland were a model for us, that we wanted to do here in Russia what they'd done in Poland, that we were asking for their help. So they agreed and played for 45 minutes; we spent the whole night in the afterglow, drinking beer . . . The pop federation lasted 10 months, until our administrator embezzled all our funds away."

*A strictly unofficial organisation of fans.

Yes, cursed money had begun to trample even our modest rock revolution. Or was it platform shoes?

'From useless victories
There remains only fatigue
If tomorrow
Promises nothing.'
        —'The Flag Upon The Castle' by Time Machine

THE PEAK OF THE 'NATIONWIDE RISE OF ROCK' came in the years 1970–72. "It was the beginning of a new decade and everyone associated this with great hopes," recalls Gradsky. In reality though, things came out rather differently. It's accepted now to think of the seventies as a 'lost' decade, as time spent asleep in a dream (for some sweet, for some nightmarish). Our rock music was also surprisingly quiet during these years, though the stormy start of the decade had seemed to promise something altogether different.

> *'Today is the very best of days,*
> *Fly the flag above the troops.*
> *Today is the very best of days,*
> *Today we make battle with fools.*
> *When the last enemy fell,*
> *The trumpet sounded victory—*
> *Only at that instant did I realize*
> *How few of us were left.'*

These lines are from a song by Time Machine called 'The Best Day' something of a rock anthem in the early seventies. And the last verse proved to be prophetic, for although no pitched battle occurred, the rock'n'roll warriors were abruptly vanquished. Dozens of bands broke up, the best clubs disappeared, and even our glorious groupies either got married or reoriented towards a more respectable clientele.

In Moscow only a dozen active groups remained. Their concerts happened without official authorisation, but on more or less professional terms, i.e. they were earning decent money for the shows. The gigs were organised by so-called 'managers' (more Anglo-Russian slang), none of whom had the slightest relation to the official concert organisations but who did have connections with the administrators of Moscow's numerous small clubs and Houses Of Culture.

This is where the underground 'sessions' took place. Organisational details were simple—you rented a hall, and distributed home-made tickets among friends and friends of friends. If we take into account the average seating capacity of the halls in question (around 400) and ticket prices anywhere from two to five roubles, we see that the revenues here were not so very small. The musicians, as a rule, got less than the 'managers', but even so the 100 plus rouble pay-days were more than they had ever dreamed of. From time to time one of the 'managers' would be apprehended and tried in court. The groups would have to testify, but fortunately avoided punishment themselves. The whole system was rather sick, but thanks to it at least some rock concerts did occur—for which we must be grateful.

There were several favourite groups in Moscow in the mid-seventies. A band led by singer-guitarist Alexey Belov called Good Buy played a repertoire of Johnny Winter, Jimi Hendrix and Robin Trower. This was the hottest and heaviest band around. Belov played the blues effortlessly and without affectation and his solos often drove the audience into a frenzy as he abused his guitar sadistically and foamed at the mouth. I knew all their songs by heart but kept going to their shows because Good Buy delivered the spirit and crazy joy of rock'n'roll. I should add that Belov didn't speak English, which somehow gave his singing an added charm. For appearance's sake Good Buy played a few jazz-rock songs of their own composition, but didn't seem to take much pleasure in them. Two other popular English-singing groups were Ruby Attack, who played a potpourri of Western hits, and Arax, who covered Beatles and Santana songs (and who later began writing songs of their own in the same style).

Then there was Leap Year Summer. As the name hints, the band appeared in the summer of 1972. The leaders were guitarist Alexander Sitkovetsky, who was enrolled in a technical college and thus had a very short haircut,* plus singer-organist Kris Kelmi, about whose hair it's difficult to say anything, since he walked around in a long blonde wig. These were serious lads.

They began by playing art rock, which was popular among fans but hadn't been heard much 'live'. Leap Year Summer worked over a few classical pieces in rock arrangements and also performed some numbers of their own with English lyrics in a style somewhere between Deep Purple and Rick Wakeman. I found myself at their first big concert, at Moscow University in the winter of 1973, more or less by accident, but immediately foresaw a big future for the group, and it was a safe prediction since at that time no one else here was playing 'cultured' rock (except for Arsenal, and they left the scene to join the philharmonia in 1976).

There's another band we can't fail to mention—Stas Namin's first group, called Flowers. Stas never pretended to be a virtuoso musician, but was a legitimate contender for the title of most effective rock 'man-

*Students in technical and economic institutes participate in military training as part of their studies, and their external appearance, accordingly, had to meet army standards.

ager' and most subtle rock politician (though wicked tongues attributed all his success to the unofficial protection afforded him by virtue of his having high-placed relatives). After going through an early copy-cat stage, Flowers soon began singing in Russian. At a time when all other rockers considered ties with the official mass media to be an utterly useless affair, Namin applied his energies precisely in that direction. Strange, but it brought results; the state record company Melodia (the only record company in the USSR) released two Flowers singles. In a certain sense, these were the first Soviet rock records. The songs were simple and sentimental, but all the same their sound and the natural quality of the vocals differed from all the VIA product coming off the conveyor.

The unquestioned number one group of the period, and not only in Moscow, was Time Machine. As performers they didn't make much of an impression—the musicianship was strictly standard and Andrey Makarevich had a nasal voice (a bit like Bob Dylan) and stilted stage manner. Their music still had an awful lot of Liverpool in it, glossed over with a hard rock veneer. Nothing special. But this was not so important, because Time Machine's real mission was different—to force people to think, i.e. think about the lyrics.

The famous and banal question, 'So how does Russian rock really differ from Western rock?' has no special answer if we speak about the music alone. To this day Russian rockers have not succeeded, despite periodic attempts, to create an independent conceptual approach to the music; from the early sixties through the mid-eighties we've made basically the same sounds as the rest of the world (though with a slight Slavic accent, of course). Neither the mid-seventies flirtation with ethnic folklore nor the recently fashionable enthusiasm for various pop music retro trends have brought any convincing results. However, if we look at the second dimension of rock, the lyrical content, we discover many differences, and fairly radical ones. The first and most influential designer of the Soviet school of rock lyrics was the ex-architectural student Andrey Makarevich.

And so, what is the difference? First of all, the lyrics in Russian rock play a more important role than in Western rock. The reasons for this may be the Russian rockers' awareness that they're borrowing music invented elsewhere, their weaker technical virtuosity, and the fact that the commercial and dancing functions of rock music never predominated here; more value was always placed on the ideas in a song. Time Machine contributed impetus to all these trends.

Second, I'll go out on a limb and assert that the purely literary level of our rock lyrics is higher, on the average, than in the West. Rock lyrics here have a direct tie to our poetic tradition and reflect its lexical and stylistic heritage. That's probably explained by the fact that 'serious' academic poetry is really very popular in the USSR. Books of verse often become bestsellers, and the most popular poets—such as Voznesensky or Yevtushenko—sometimes read their works in sold out sports palaces, just like rock stars. In the late fifties we already had a recognised school of bard performers, poet intellectuals who sang their verses and played an acoustic guitar accompaniment. Makarevich's rock was a direct heir and continuation of that tradition, though in a modernised version, of course.

Third, our rockers don't sing about the same things that Western rockers do (which flows from the second point). In the entire enormous repertoire of Time Machine there's not a single clear-cut love song, let alone one about sex. Closest of all would be their famous blues number 'You Or I':

> 'Everything's very simple—fairytales or deceit,
> The sunny island disappears in fog,
> Earth has no castles in the sky,
> Someone was mistaken—you or I.'

So what, then, did our first rock poet (and his myriad successors) sing about? About social and ethical issues. Human indifference, for instance:

> 'Here is my house, windows shut tight,
> Let the whole world turn upside down,
> My house will preserve me.'

Or social passivity:

> 'You never chose a path
> And had nothing to do.
> You didn't find what you sought
> And didn't seek what you desired.'

Conformism:

> 'A wave will pass right by someone like you,
> And somehow you always go unnoticed.
> Even if some blame will fall on each of us,
> There'll be nothing to blame on you.'

Or hypocrisy:

> 'Behind a mask you're invisible,
> Like someone in a fairytale,
> And you can laugh at your friends
> As much as you want.'

And so forth. To my taste, Makarevich's lyrics are a bit bland—abstract and didactic. But they're unquestionably honest and full of concern. And they give an accurate picture, even if in a somewhat dull focus, of the symptoms of a nasty epidemic of selfishness and lack of faith that infected one and all at that time. Naturally, some considered it wrong to talk about such things out loud for everyone to hear, and the mass media worked hard at maintaining a thoroughly cheery (and false) image of an infallible, ideologically committed contemporary hero. Time Machine's 'problematic' songs got a strong response precisely for this reason. I remember in the spring of 1978 we travelled together to a big student songfest in Sverdlovsk, and it was amazing to find that the audience there knew all of Makarevich's songs by heart, although the group had never played previously in those parts.

There was another strong response as well. At the same Sverdlovsk festival I was a member of the judging committee and got to observe at close range the massive shock suffered by the local officials, brought on by Time Machine's lyrics. They were especially shocked by a satirical anti-alcohol blues number called 'The Unmitigated Damage Of Drunkenness' and by another song called 'The Calm', with the following lines:

'My ship is a creation of able hands,
My course is a total disaster.
But just let the wind pick up
And everything around will change,
Including the idiot who thinks otherwise.
An answer ready for every question,
Night has always made right,
But no one believes that
There's no wind on earth,
Even if they've banned the wind.'

Time Machine was disqualified from the competition. Though they were clearly the best group there, the bureaucrats were afraid to affix their signatures to such a recognition. The band had found itself in similar situations before—they were constantly accused of 'pessimism' and a 'decadent mentality' and 'distorting the image of our youth'.

The indignation of the cultural authorities was compounded by the fact that our pop music, traditionally, had always been the most simplistic and superficial branch of artistic propaganda. Thus there was something of a double standard in operation—the same degree of criticism that was deemed OK for, say, the press was not permissible in a pop song. For example, once I was on the judging committee for a competition of political songs, and one group from Novosibirsk broke up the usual flow of anti-war and anti-fascist songs by performing an exposé on the Soviet *nouveau riche* black market speculators. There was a panic, and though I tried to explain to my comrades on the judging committee that the lyrics for the song were taken from a well-known poem by Yevgeny Yevtushenko that had recently been published in the newspaper *Komsomolskaya Pravda* (circulation of about 10 million copies), it was no use. The satire was declared a provocation.

Official pop music, meanwhile, didn't allow itself anything at all. A decade earlier the scene had at least been lively, but the seventies gave us nothing worth remembering. Just a multitude of depressing bands (The Gems, Flame, Singing Hearts, Blue Guitars), each one worse than the last, and performers using the same mannerisms practised since the post-war years, i.e. the same buttoned-up suits, the same expressionless faces, brightened only occasionally by a poster-style smile (usually during the choruses). There were only two exceptions—Alla Pugachova, former vocalist of The Jolly Kids, who at least resembled a real live woman and sang about the trials and tribulations of love, and David Tukhmanov, a professional composer already in his thirties who, unlike the other craftsmen of 'easy listening', had an inkling of certain new trends and as a result recorded two 'concept' albums of quasi-rock entitled 'The World Is So Beautiful' and 'The Waves Of My Memory'. The formula for both was more or less the same: modern electric arrangements, guest 'underground' rock soloists (including Gradsky and Mekhrdada Badi, the Iranian vocalist from Arsenal), and the use of classical verses from the likes of Goethe and Baudelaire as lyrics. I can't say that Tukhmanov's songs were really strong, but compared to the unbelievably pathetic pop product options then available, his albums seemed like a real achievement and were bought up in record quantities by the music-starved youth.

Real rock music, meanwhile, continued to languish in obscurity. The first more or less objective articles about Western bands began to appear in the press, but the local scene still got no recognition and no publicity, let alone any chances to release records. The whole genre was surrounded by a wall of silence, or a tall fence (to use one of Makarevich's metaphors). Thinking musicians were wondering to themselves—why bother to engage in this at all if there's no solution in sight? In addition, playing rock'n'roll was becoming too expensive a pastime for amateurs. Using worn out home-made equipment and low quality instruments was both unaesthetic and uncool. But Western equipment, which was available only on the black market, fetched amazing prices. The market was supplied mainly by bands from Yugoslavia, Poland, etc. who would sell off all their gear at the end of a Soviet tour and receive two or three times more than what it was worth in their own country. A Fender or Gibson electric guitar went for three to five thousand roubles, and I often heard Moscow musicians say, "Why should I buy a guitar (or organ)? Better to get a car, or just live for a few years on the money."

The word 'rok' means bad fate in Russian, and it really seemed that rock music was doomed. A corresponding mood began to come through in newly-written songs, which, naturally, only made the genre that much more suspicious and undesirable in official eyes. The pathos of alienation was expressed in the majority of Time Machine songs:

'You still don't believe that we're forgotten
And you break down doors though your hands are broken.
You're disarmed and superfluous,
There's nothing left but the night and winter frost.'

It was shared by the other oracles of the younger generation in those years. A Leningrad group called The Myths, headed by an excellent singer and guitarist named Yuri Ilchenko, played melancholy songs about life on the street and worked for years on completing their magnum opus, a rock opera called 'The Jingle Of Coins', about how cynicism ruins young people. In the end Ilchenko got fed up knocking at doors that no one would open and he left The Myths for a professional philharmonia (to earn some coins).

Things were even worse for the complete lack of verifiable information on what was happening around us. The rock community here was much better informed about the situation in England or the USA, thanks to records and radio, than about the rock scene in neighbouring Soviet cities. Certain ties existed between Moscow and Leningrad— Time Machine were exceptionally popular in Leningrad, and The Myths played a few times for us in Moscow—but the rest of the country was *terra incognita*. Thus it was a big surprise when I discovered a remarkable student avant-garde group in Sverdlovsk called Sonance, led by Alexander Pantikin, that played unorthodox instrumental rock that reminded one of Shostakovich or Prokofiev.

And my first visit to Estonia, at the end of 1975, was a real shock. I travelled with Alexey Belov and Good Buy for a festival at the Tallin Polytechnic Institute, and everything there was different—they had rock traditions and a real rock 'culture'. After Belov sang 'Blue Suede Shoes' in his typical sloppy style, a whole crowd of dispirited Estonians approached him backstage to ask how he could dare sing a classic song like that without the slightest understanding of the lyrics. Belov was surprised by the question, since he had never encountered such a reaction in the capital.

The best thing about Estonian rock was the variety of styles. In Russia everything was concentrated in two areas—hard rock, and the Time Machine style, which acquired the nickname 'bard rock'. But here there was everything—Apelsin, with singer Ivo Linna, played country music and rockabilly; Sven Grunberg and his band Mees meditated via their home-made synthesisers while a small fountain gurgled to one side of the stage; Rein Rannap and his band Ruya performed monumental compositions with a national flavour using a large vocal chorus; the long-haired drummer Paap Kilar conducted a symphony orchestra that accompanied his fusion band Psycho. It was all unbelievably impressive and unexpected—like Tallin's Latin script and gothic architecture. The dazed Russians in attendance walked around thoughtfully whispering to themselves about 'the West . . .' But this was not the West by a long shot; it's just that in Estonia rock had developed under normal conditions and had been more or less painlessly integrated into the artistic life of the republic. In the summer there were even free festivals in the town of Vilyandi, where hippies gathered from all across the country.

I don't know just why things happened that way in Estonia. In neighbouring Latvia, which was no less 'Western', the situation was exactly the opposite—a severe policy by the cultural establishment drove a once lively rock scene to a pathetic state. Pete Anderson gave up playing rock for 10 years, as there was no one to play with, nowhere to play, and nothing to play for. In Lithuania there were no decent groups, although there were rock operas being staged in numerous theatres.

So, in each city the situation was a little different, and no one knew what their neighbours were up to. The absence of any communication among the various rock centres put me in a unique position; thanks to my articles in the Soviet press I'd acquired something of a name, and was receiving correspondence and invitations from everywhere. It would have been a sin not to take advantage of the situation, and I decided to make a change from passive journalism to active networking. The simplest and most effective way to bring musicians from different cities together was through a festival. I began working on it and soon found backers among some young scientists in the town of Noginsk, about 20 kilometres east of Moscow, near the centre for cosmonaut training. They had a cosy 800-seat concert hall, a hotel and a little money to pay for the participants' travel expenses. The rest depended on my connections.

None of the high-level official organisations showed any interest in the festival (Oh happy, sleepy days!) so we managed to avoid bureaucratic red tape and all arrangements were made in six weeks. The festival happened in October 1978. The featured performers were Time Machine and Leap Year Summer, both of whom were at the peak of their form, plus several other Moscow bands since forgotten. The guests from distant parts included Sonance (Sverdlovsk), Magnetic Band (Estonia) and two remarkable bards—the Lithuanian, Virgis Stakenas, enormous, bearded, and sensuous like Leonard Cohen, and Harald Simanis, a Latvian gypsy and tiler by profession who sang in an odd, deep falsetto and accompanied himself on the organ. In retrospect it seems that I managed to get together all the acts I knew that I considered interesting.

The festival had a judging committee, of course. This is a phenomenon of all our musical get-togethers; a commission of esteemed individuals whose presence adds respectability to the affair. It also serves as a pretext for presenting the participants with all sorts of certificates and awards (which were important for Soviet rock musicians, since such pieces of paper were the only tangible symbols of official recognition they were likely to receive in the absence of any press coverage, gold albums, and so forth).

The judging committee at Noginsk was headed by the jazz composer and all-round good guy Yuri Saulsky (whose son played keyboards in various Moscow pop bands). First prize awards went to Time Machine, Virgis Stakenas and Magnetic Band. The latter group was led by singer and drummer Gunnar Graps, who played previously in the psychedelic bands Coma and Ornament but had by this time switched to funky blues with a dash of virtuoso flourish. Magnetic Band had experienced some problems in Estonia, apparently due to some *risqué* lyrics, but as soon as Graps brought home his prize from Moscow, his band was invited to join the philharmonia.

I spent the end of the festival lying on the floor in a café where all the musicians had gathered to play a farewell improvised session. The keynote number, as always, was an endless blues jam.

My story about the troubled seventies would be incomplete without mentioning certain events of international importance. Detente brought us not only the Apollo-Soyuz space project and cigarettes of the same name, but some tours by American country and jazz bands as well (including The Nitty Gritty Dirt Band). The charming B.B. King invited his Soviet audience to the banks of the Mississippi, and Boney M, a disco-reggae band from West Germany and the new favourites of the day, gave two lip-sync concerts for a privileged crowd. (Tickets went for 150 roubles on the black market and one of the Deputy Ministers Of Culture was sacked for speculating with them.)

The big musical scandal of the decade was the cancellation of an open Soviet-American rock festival in Leningrad on July 4, 1978. Santana, Joan Baez and The Beach Boys were the expected guest stars, and their arrival had been announced not only over Voice Of America but also in the Leningrad newspapers. Fans from all over the country gathered on Palace Square, but found no one there save a crowd of militiamen. It turned out that the whole undertaking fell apart a few days before the holiday, but no one took the trouble to warn people. Thousands of bewildered fans loitered around Nevsky Prospekt all evening, chanting 'San-ta-na!' and bumping up against the militia cordons. By nightfall everyone had dispersed.

At the end of May 1979, Elton John came to the USSR, the first visit by a big Western rock star. The stage design and sound quality were stunning, though the performance itself was a bit disappointing,

The roots of Estonian rock: The Optimists, in 1964, looking anything but.

The roots of Leningrad rock: The Avanguard, featuring Yacheslav Mastiev – the local Elvis – on vocals.

Alexey Kozlov, thirty years on from his days as a *stilyagi*.

Saint Petersburg, the first Leningrad rock band to sing in their native tongue, in 1972.

Pete Anderson, wearing glasses, among the first Soviet performers, with his group The Melody Makers in 1966.

A nameless Red Army rock band expressing themselves in the barracks.

Mike Naumenko (left) and Swine in 1982.

Alexey Belov, of The Good Buy, and a colleague at the author's birthday party in Moscow in 1975.

Sergei Kuryokhin, keyboard player with Pop Mechanics, with the author during his 1982 bearded period.

Alexander Davydov, former leader of Strange Games, who died of a drug overdose in June 1984.

The Leningrad Rock Club audience. Kolya Vasin, the famous Soviet 'Beatleologist' is sat in the third row, fifth from left, with a beard. (Where are the girls? Ed.)

Andrey Makarevich receiving the first prize at the Tbilisi '80 Festival which, like all major rock events in Russia, was treated as a competition in a similar manner to the Eurovision Song Contest. On the right is jury chairman Yuri Saulsky.

Aquarium's finest hour: Mikhail Vasilyev, Boris Grebenschikov and Andrey Romanov (left to right) on stage at the Tbilisi '80 Festival.

An early shot of Bravo featuring Zhanna Aguzarova on vocals.

Alexander Bashlachev, the new northern rock bard who has been described by the author as the 'singing Dostoyevsky'.

Sipoli; Martins Braun is second from right.

Yuri Chernavsky, the mad professor of Soviet electronic rock.

Alexander Gradsky, who spans three decades of Soviet rock, in concert in 1987.

Night Avenue in concert.

Mike Naumenko, of the far sighted lyrics and uncompromising delivery, probably singing 'You Bitch'.

The acceptable face of Soviet rock: The Stas Namin Group who, like Autograph, have become an export band. Namin is standing second from left.

Hardy Volmer, of Turist, gypsy dancing at the Tartu '84 festival.

I think. It was not real rock music—just Elton behind a white Steinway (in a floppy cap and pseudo-sharovari*) with Ray Cooper on percussion. Still, it was an event, and the weather in Moscow was magnificent. After the final concert of the tour Gradsky and I got backstage, hoping to talk with the musicians, and found ourselves at a small banquet in pure decadent, superstar style—everyone was drinking French champagne straight from the bottle and pouring it over each others' heads between gulps. I decided to give it a try—for Soviet rock and for the new decade—so I took a big swig . . . and poured what was left in the bottle all over a small, stocky man with a short beard who turned out to be Harvey Goldsmith.

*Old-fashioned Ukranian baggy trousers.

5.

'So where are the young punks
That will sweep us
From the face of the earth?'
—'Young Punks' by Aquarium.

ONCE MY MOTHER BURST IN ON ME, frightened by the noise coming from my room and thinking something was wrong with her son—but it was just Alan Vega singing 'Frankie Teardrop'. New Wave brought me a change in consciousness—I divorced my wife the hippie and, after listening to 'No New York', began writing unanswered letters to Lydia Lunch (to be honest, I wrote two in all). I felt younger and began dancing again, but at the same time it was a bit unreal since there was no hint of a new wave in our music in the late seventies. Hard rock and bard rock and fusion were thriving, bell-bottom pants and platform shoes were in fashion . . . all of which was less than stimulating.

My strongest recollections from that period are the concerts of Vyacheslav Ganelin's trio (the Marx Brothers of free jazz, as I called them in an article). They were at their peak and making the most passionate, inventive, caustic music around. Formally they were distant from rock—no electric instruments, purely instrumental compositions—but their concerts were infinitely more lively and challenging than anything being done by the electric groups. (It's a pity that the Western public discovered Ganelin, Tarasov and Chekasin only later, already in a stage of fatigue and dissension.)

To my stock, desperate question: "Have you heard of any berserk new groups lately?" all answers were negative. "What do you mean, anyway?" people would counter; "Who needs that?" Only some acquaintances from Estonia had any intriguing reports, but one of their bands, New Drain Pipes, proved on close inspection to be just another derivative effort from the restaurant milieu, while Propeller, 'the real thing', came to my attention only much later.

There are various reasons why punk and new wave (unlike, say, progressive rock) took so long to break through in the USSR. A psychological reason: having always been put down as a poor cousin of 'real' (high) culture, our rockers humbly strove for symbols of 'prestige', meaning complex musical arrangements, technical virtuosity, poetic lyrics or even just chic costumery. The anarchic, consciously seedy pathos of 1977 was alien to our musicians. Whereas Johnny Rotten might take it as a sign of his street credibility to have grown-ups call him a hooligan, our rockers had been branded that way for ages for no reason, and wanted only to rid themselves of such appellations.

Another reason was that our listeners had an acute case of disco fixation. Teenagers who only recently had idolised Deep Purple, Slade and Sweet now couldn't live without Boney M and Donna Summer.

The only thing anyone knew about punks was that they were 'fascists', because that's how our British-based correspondents had described them for us. Several angry feature articles appeared in the summer and fall of 1977 with lurid descriptions of their unsavoury appearance and disgraceful manners, including one that quoted sympathetically a diatribe from the *Daily Telegraph*. (It took punk to get their positions together.) To illustrate all this, a few photos of 'monsters' with swastikas were printed.

In the bibliography of Soviet articles about rock there are three entries on The Sex Pistols, and their titles are 'How To Fight Against Hooliganism', 'Decked Out In Brown' and 'The Swindle Machine'. Attempts to show that punk was not a creation of the National Front met with no success, even when supported by quotes from *The Morning Star* and excerpts of Clash lyrics. The image of punks as Nazis was established very effectively, and in our country, as you should understand, the swastika will *never* receive a positive reaction, even purely for shock value. (Unfortunately, punk's image hasn't really changed to this day; I remember how nervous some of our komsomol bosses got recently at Billy Bragg's concert in Leningrad when he told the audience that he had started out in a punk group.)

But I see the main reason for punk rock's failure here as something different. In the Russian understanding of music, which I mentioned in connection with The Beatles, we have no tradition of playing loud and fast and dirty. Maybe our love for melody and a 'clean' sound is embedded in the genes. How else can one explain the boundless love for a miserable group like Smokie or the enormous popularity of The Eagles in the late seventies . . . and the total disregard for The Sex Pistols, although everyone knew of their odious name.

Both the 'informed' collectors and rock musicians themselves shared the negative view of punk. At his concerts Makarevich began ceremoniously dedicating a song to punks with the words:

> 'You can walk around like a garden,
> Gone to seed, or shave it bald,
> I've seen both those numbers before . . .'

"Have you ever actually seen a single punk?" I asked him, upset by such demagogy. He didn't answer, but looked at me intently, apparently giving me to understand that he thought he was hearing all this from none other than a punk. People accused me of snobbery, exclaiming sincerely, "After all, you can't *like* the music!"

Western journalists often ask me about Soviet punk, and when I answer that for all practical purposes we have no punk rock, they don't believe it and look at me as if I'm maliciously concealing some treasure or just afraid to divulge 'secret' information. "It can't be," they say. "We've heard that you have such groups, but they're banned, of course . . ." OK, let's put it this way: we don't have any groups that play punk rock as it's known in the West. There are bands with a 'punkish' approach to lyrics, and bands that never come out of their basements, but they all play heavy metal, electropop, even folk rock, but nothing like punk. Punk rock with us is something exotic, like an avocado—everyone has heard the name, but very few know what it actually is.

The rare exceptions (which will be discussed in detail) only confirm the rule. It's possible that the situation will change, but that's about as likely as The Beatles cult ever passing away.

Let's return to Moscow, fall of 1979. Noginsk-II was going ahead at full speed, and this time everything was on a more serious scale—16 groups from six cities. Some of them I hadn't heard before, but chose intuitively based on hazy rumours and recommendations. Both the volume of work and the interest towards the festival were much greater than a year before. My monthly salary (130 roubles) didn't even cover expenses for long distance telephone calls. The situation with tickets was a catastrophe—I had an enormous folder of applications from newspapers, magazines, radio and TV requesting accreditation and a spot in the hall. In the end the applications weren't needed (the folder is stashed away somewhere in a drawer at home) because the festival was cancelled two days before it was to start.

For some unknown reason (most likely in the hope of earning some extra expression of gratitude, or maybe just for insurance's sake) the brothers from Noginsk took all their documentation on the festival to the First Secretary of the Moscow city komsomol committee, who immediately registered surprise upon reading through the list of participants.

"A festival of vocal-instrumental groups, you say? Somehow I don't recognise any of the names . . . for instance, Kon Tiki—where is that group from?"

"From the First Medical Institute . . ."

There immediately followed a call to the komsomol committee at the institute, and the people there answered that they knew nothing of Kon Tiki. (Maybe they were frightened by the voice of such high-ranking officialdom or maybe they really didn't know.) "So you see, comrades—even in their own institute no one knows your group," came the reply. "And you want to put them in a festival! No, I can't authorise such a festival."

I don't think that the First Secretary was genuinely as uninformed as he claimed to be, since the list of festival participants contained some fairly well-known groups, including Time Machine. Perhaps it was just this that frightened him and brought about his little scenario. The sad thing is that his permission was not required; there was no need to go and OK anything. But once the head of the capital city's komsomol had refused, the local activists couldn't disobey.

It was quite cheering to hear about all this over the telephone that evening. I managed to warn some of the groups, literally hours before their trains departed, but others were already en route. Colleagues from the magazine *Student Meridian* helped organise an alternative site (a 300-seat conference hall on the 20th floor of the Young Guard Publishing House) and quite unexpectedly, this ceremony of mourning for refugees from the-festival-that-never-was turned into one of the best rock concerts Moscow has ever seen. The carefree capital saw and heard what it hadn't even dreamed existed—a Soviet new wave, in the form of Aquarium and Sipoli.

Aquarium's appearance at the festival happened like this. Since all of the more or less famous Leningrad groups at that time (Earth Men, Rossiyanye, The Argonauts) were pretty awful, I asked Andrey Makarevich if there weren't any unknown but original bands there. (Time Machine travelled to Leningrad almost every month.) "Probably only Aquarium," he answered. "They play pretty, acoustic songs, with a flute and cello . . . The lyrics are interesting, sort of philosophical." I can't say this recommendation inspired me much, but I called Aquarium's leader Boris Grebenschikov on the phone and asked him straight, "What do you play?" He began listing some of his favourite musicians and mentioned, among others, Lou Reed. It was the first time in my life I had heard Lou Reed's name from the mouth of a Russian rock musician. Velvet Underground were unknown here. I was intrigued, and the issue was decided; "OK, Boris, buy your tickets."

Onto the stage stepped six musicians, aged 25 to 26. Boris with guitar, a rhythm section, cello, flute and bassoon. They were dressed a bit ragged, in faded jeans, t-shirts and wrinkled jackets. Their stage manner was loose, laughing and chattering among themselves. When the singer put on thin black glasses to tune his guitar, the audience sat up straight—all this seemed to resemble the notorious punk. "Our group belongs to the Dom Kulturi of a metallurgical factory. We play for workers, and they like our music." So began their concert, and I began counting the influences in their music. Dylanesque talking folk rock and soft songs in the style of Cat Stevens; monotone rock *à la* the

Velvets and one remarkable, melodic medieval ballad to the words of Thomas Malory (*Morte D'Arthur*) that Steeleye Span would have been proud of. Here was a band of knowledgeable rock fans, and I immediately accepted them as soul brothers, because their frank eclecticism was so much more inspiring than the rigid conservatism of most of our rock groups. Aquarium was opening a new world of influences to the many people (including musicians) who had barely a hazy idea of rock music beyond the familiar confines of Beatles-Led Zeppelin-Rick Wakeman-Chicago. But even more important were the lyrics. On the one hand, they were written with a talented poetic touch—as good as Makarevich—and pretty images, such as:

> '*It seems I recognise myself*
> *In the little boy reading verses.*
> *He grabs the hands of the clock*
> *So that the night won't end,*
> *And blood flows from his hand.*'

On the other hand, they were closer to rock lyrics as I understood them, i.e. down to earth, ironic, with simple conversational language. The first song Aquarium played was 'Simple Man's Blues'.

> '*Yesterday I was walking home,*
> *Spring was everywhere,*
> *I met him on the corner, but*
> *Couldn't figure him at all.*
> *He asked me, "To be or not to be?"*
> *I told him to go get . . .*'

Grebenschikov's semi-rude slang sounded to my ears like a chorus of angels. Finally I was hearing in Russian what I'd heard for so long in English. Of course the influences (Dylan, Reed, Morrison) were fairly transparent, but they were the right influences! Aquarium finished their set with 'Did You See The Flying Saucer?' with the final line:

> '*If I were the saucer, I'd*
> *Never fly over Petrozavodsk.*'*

*Soviet city north of Leningrad where UFO sightings were reported at the time.

Such was the debut of Aquarium, the group that has largely set the tone of Soviet rock in the eighties. I was happy to have a new child on my hands (more like a difficult adolescent). The crowd was perplexed. A group of relieved colleagues from Noginsk walked up to me and said that they would have had troubles if Aquarium had played at their festival.

Last up was Sipoli. The story of their appearance is similar to that of Aquarium. A friend from Riga, the high society vagabond and eminent disc jockey Karlis, relayed me the following information. "It's a good group, an excellent group." He couldn't explain anything more specific. Sipoli was chosen for two reasons. First, because I had already heard almost all the Latvian groups (Credo, Inversion, Livi and others) at a festival just that summer in Liepaja and none had made much of an impression on me; second, there was a story circulating that one of Sipoli's songs had caused a scandal on Latvian radio, and that was certainly something promising. (It turned out that the song in question was 'Harlem', with lyrics from a poem by Langston Hughes in which there was a line to the effect that 'prices went up again in the grocery', and the touchy local authorities took it as a complaint in their direction.)

Sipoli played a short set, three or four songs, that stood the crowd on its head. It was high energy rhythm'n'blues, but with an unusual vocal arrangement (two male voices, one female) and melodic lines that reminded one more of Kurt Weill or Karl Orff than of black music. Their last song, 'Hey Hey Blues', tore through the hall like a tornado —a driving, tense, crazy-happy number that summed up the general mood and served as a worthy finale to the whole concert. Sipoli's music bore no relation to Western new wave, but it was energetic and original and such qualities, as they say in the Levi's jeans ad, never go out of style.

When I became better acquainted with Martin Brauns, the manic keyboard player and singer of Sipoli (the name means onions in Latvian), I learned that he had graduated from the Riga Conservatory and that his main occupation was composing scores for films and theatre productions. It was astonishing to think that someone with a conservatory education had remained a real rocker, sincere and straightforward. The only way his diploma helped him was in smoothing over various conflicts that his eccentric and capricious personality got him into, whereupon just a word about his being a graduate of the conservatory and a member of the Union Of Composers would exercise a magically calming effect on any and all bureaucrats. "A rather repellent practice," he admitted later.

The concert in question had no negative consequences, but the near future held in store an event of even grander proportions.

If you ask fans here to name the most important event in Soviet rock history, I believe most are likely to choose the Tbilisi* festival of 1980, and it's probably an accurate choice. Tbilisi-80 was the largest and most representative of all our festivals. There were philharmonia groups, restaurant groups, Dom Kulturi and 'underground' groups, groups from Moscow, Leningrad, the Ukraine, Pribaltika, Caucasus and Central Asia. Only Siberia was unrepresented. One article in a Western newspaper compared Spring Rhythms (the festival's official name) to Woodstock, but there was little resemblance. Tbilisi-80 took place in March,

*Capital city of Soviet Georgia.

53

in cold weather, in a 2000-seat concert hall of the Georgian Philharmonia, and the performances were rated by a judging committee. (Imagine an official judging committee and prize winners at Woodstock!)
The one thing the festivals did have in common is that each proved to
be both a grand culmination of the movement it expressed (the American counter culture and Soviet 'unofficial' rock) and at the same time
the beginning of its commercial degeneration.

The story of the Tbilisi rock festival began one evening in September
1979 at the Sofia, a fairly nasty little restaurant in the centre of Moscow
on Mayakovsky Square. Despite the bad food, uninteresting crowd and
exceptionally boorish, perpetually drunk, occasionally even pugnacious
waiters, we went there often because Alexey Belov and the remnants
of The Good Buy played as house band.

Sitting there one evening at a long table with a large group, I had
a talk with Gayoz Kandelaky, assistant director of the Georgian Philharmonia. Adventurous and cavalier, like the majority of Georgians,
he also possessed a European business sense and purposefulness, which
he had demonstrated amply in organising an excellent jazz festival in
1978. Our conversation went along lines to the effect that rock seemed
to be on the rise, the philharmonias were flirting with the amateur
groups, the mass media were clamouring for seats at the upcoming
festival (this was before Noginsk-II fell apart in November), Time Machine were playing in the prestigious Union Of Composers Hall, and
so forth. At which point Gayoz said, "What do you say we organise a
big festival in Tbilisi in the spring? You know that I like jazz more,
but we could give rock a try." Belov's group received an invitation on
the spot.

One has to know Georgians so as not to immediately take on faith
all such proposals made in the expansive mood that comes over a few
bottles of wine. But the next day we continued our negotiations in a
restaurant outside Moscow called Saltikovka.

A new group, Carnival, was playing there and they too were invited
to Tbilisi, though it turned out later that the restaurant's manager
wouldn't release them for the festival. (The two leaders of Carnival,
Alexander Barykin and Vladimir Kuzmin, became big pop stars, and
big rivals, in the mid-eighties.) Gayoz and I agreed that I would take
responsibility for recruiting groups from Moscow, Leningrad and Pribaltika, plus the press and a Moscow section for the judging committee.
And on that we parted until March 7, the day before the festival opened.

And so, Tbilisi . . . I'll quote a lyrical excerpt from the liner notes
I wrote for a double album recorded at the festival and released on
Melodia a year later:

'Spring in Tbilisi was cold and cloudy. The sun shone rarely and
a freezing rain fell from time to time, as if adding the finishing
touches to a quaint but slightly melancholy scene of a city between

seasons. But the peaceful streets pulsed with a certain vibration, whose epicentre was a round, glass structure housing the Grand concert hall. Volga and Zhiguli automobiles scurried around the service entrance throughout the day, dropping off and picking up people whom the passers-by eyed wth lively interest . . . "The bands!" The vibration reached its peak in the evening, when excited crowds of young people streamed towards the building from all sides. Some of them were looking for tickets, and when none could be found they considered storming the fragile glass doors in desperation.

'Around midnight an electrified crowd flowed out of the hall and wandered about the sleeping city for hours, illuminating its chilly streets with the tracer lights of their cigarettes. As a TASS correspondent reported from the scene, "The capital of Soviet Georgia is in the grips of a musical fever." '

To this introduction we should add a few well-known facts. Tbilisi is a fantastically beautiful and engaging city, with buildings so strange and exotic one can't tell whether they were built 50 or 500 years ago . . . a mass of cars and anarchic traffic . . . liquor stores open until midnight . . . little in common with Russia at all. Tbilisi is also a very prosperous city. In those days, long black leather coats were the fashion in Georgia and the entire population of Tbilisi—men and women, composers and *kolkhozniki**—was decked out in them (price: around 1,000 roubles each).

*Collective farm workers.

But the main thing about Tbilisi is its hospitality. All the improbable legends you may have heard about Georgian hospitality are almost certainly true. One thing very few people have heard about is that I put on 10 kilograms during my 10 days in Tbilisi at that time, despite all the hustle and bustle connected with the festival. Moreover, I didn't visit a single restaurant (the restaurants in Tbilisi are mediocre). Every night after the concerts our hosts packed us into automobiles and took us to their homes, where we stayed until four or five in the morning. I had a tough time getting up each day at noon . . . while in the meantime Gayoz, Rudiko, Bichi and other local friends had been at work all morning. And so it went each day and each night. The endurance of Tbilisi's social lions was absolutely amazing.

As to the music, it was less enchanting than the evening parties. The concerts were not bad, just rather predictable. Of eight Georgian groups, seven played fusion or bad hard rock. Only Blitz made a strong impression. Several rock veterans and leading local bohemians (a painter, a sculptor, and a karate expert) got together two weeks before the festival and pasted together a programme of short songs reminiscent of The Beatles but with a light Caucasian flavour and simple new wave arrangements somewhat like Blondie or early Elvis Costello. They were dressed amusingly (gold caftans, soldier boots, ski caps) and had an offhand stage manner that was vastly refreshing against the background of studied seriousness projected by the other groups.

"We didn't know up to the last day whether they'd let us play at the festival or not," Blitz's leader and guitarist, Valery Kocharov, told me later, "and we couldn't have cared less. All these prizes and certificates, who needs them? We just wanted to have a good time and keep cool . . ." As a result of which, Blitz won the Audience's Favourite prize. For me they were the only find at the festival.

(Valery Kocharov continues his work as a sculptor and simultaneously continues Blitz, through whose ranks have passed more than 20 musicians. Sometimes they tour with a repertoire exclusively of Beatles songs; the costume department of Tbilisi's opera theatre made them outfits with exact copies of the jackets on the 'Sgt. Pepper' cover. Many times I've tried to talk Kocharov into rehearsing his own songs and getting into the Soviet rock movement, especially since nothing else worthwhile has appeared in Georgia to this day, but he answers that he enjoys singing Beatles songs most and the rest interests him little. Valery is a really colourful figure, the most independent-minded, self-willed artist I know—having a lot of money undoubtedly helps him here—as well as the most berserk driver I've ever seen behind the wheel of an automobile. On top of that, he asserts in all seriousness that he's the direct descendant of a Chinese imperial dynasty!)

The chairman of the Tbilisi festival judging committee was the inevitable and irreplaccable Yuri Salsky, and first place prizes went to Time Machine and Magnetic Band. Everything was just as it had been in the autumn of 1978. When I brought this up with Gunnar Graps he happily exclaimed, "That's how it's going to be now for the next five years." It seemed like the truth, too, and put me in a melancholy mood, evoking thoughts of a new 'establishment' which could lead to stagnation and decline. All the more so since both Makarevich and Graps had executed an unmistakable turn towards popular taste. The experimental, funky numbers had disappeared completely from Magnetic Band's show, and they were now playing pure r'n'b with one reggae song thrown in. Time Machine were performing 'New Turn', a pre-packaged, suitable-for-restaurant standard completely lacking a message, something rare for Makarevich. (I had a long laugh reading in one Western article—or was it in a thick book—that 'New Turn' was a courageous new Soviet rock song challenging the leadership to take a new course.)

Second place went to Autograph, a brand new Moscow group that no one had heard before the festival. I hadn't heard them either (although I had assured the organisers that I'd attended one of their rehearsals and that it was superb). In fact there was no great risk in this, since Autograph was none other than the new creation of Alexander Sitkovetsky, from the remnants of Leap Year Summer, and Alexander is one of Moscow's most fundamentally sound rockers. He'd already been rehearsing the new band behind closed doors for six months. Autograph offered the technocratic side of rock—well composed, flawlessly played but more or less devoid of feeling. While Leap Year Summer had retained a touch of rock's time honoured sloppy spontaneity, Autograph's musical structure was so strict as to allow no loopholes for improvisation. Their attack was tight and powerful, but it was interesting to note that after their set the judging committee applauded longer than the rest of the audience, while in most cases it had been the other way around.

The rest of the awards went to pompous art rock groups—Dialogue (Ukraine), Labyrinth (Georgia), Time (Gorky) and to Integral, a band from Saratov that played everything from country music to jazz rock, with the feel of a restaurant floor show.

As to my new wave favourites, it turned out they had 'arrived too soon' and were not understood (to put it mildly). Sipoli couldn't finish their set due to equipment problems, and what they did manage to play, an expressionist suite called 'Ode To A Scorpion', was evaluated by the judges as an interesting but 'anti-humanist' piece (about the end of civilisation after nuclear war, when scorpions and other such creatures inherit the earth). Sipoli's flop upset Martin Brauns so much that he went on a desperate binge (not hard to do in Tbilisi) and disappeared from sight. The festival was soon buzzing with the story of a raving rocker who woke up his entire hotel late one night with pistol shots. Almost nobody believed the story, figuring it was pure Georgian fantasy. In fact, it was Martin, and the 'weapon' was a small starting pistol that Sipoli used in one of their songs.

Aquarium also won no laurels at the festival, but managed to create *their* scandal right in the concert hall (and without resorting to firearms). The group played one of the best concerts of their career; there was more electric rock than in their Moscow concert, and several excellent new songs appeared: 'Piece Of Life' ('Give me my piece of life, before I'm gone from here'), 'Heroes' ('Sometimes I think we're heroes, backs to the wall, afraid of no one; sometimes I think we're just dirt'), and 'Minus 30', probably my favourite from Aquarium's repertoire, a midtempo number built on a hypnotic riff and ritualistic vocal build up influenced perhaps by the work of Jim Morrison and Patti Smith.

> *'Today there's snow on the street.*
> *It's minus 30, if the announcer's not lying.*
> *My bed is cold as ice, but*
> *This is not the time to sleep.*
> *Only the dead could sleep in this place.*
> *Forward, forward!*
> *I don't ask for good, and don't seek evil.*
> *Today I'm among you again, in search of warmth.'*

The girlfriend I was with in Tbilisi at the time knew little about rock music but was knowledgeable about theatre. The concerts were fairly boring for her, poor thing, but Aquarium caught her eye. "This is almost Brecht," she said approvingly.

*Nickname of a popular café and hangout in Leningrad.

> 'And when I stand in the Saigon*
> People come in on their own two wheels.
> The big shots come in big cars
> But I don't want to be one of them.'

Against the background of our relatively respectable rockers, Aquarium looked like a real band of rebels. When Boris began stroking his guitar against the microphone stand and then lay down on the stage holding his (borrowed) Telecaster on his stomach and clanging on the strings, the entire judging committee stood up and demonstratively left the hall, as if to say, "We bear no responsibility for the performance of such hooligans." The concert, meanwhile, carried on. The cellist Seva hoisted his instrument atop the still supine Boris and began hacking with his bow while the bassoonist circled them, gesturing with his sinister looking instrument as if shooting the entire outrageous deformity. Georgia hadn't seen the likes of this before; half the audience applauded furiously, while the other half whistled in indignation.

All this, though, was nothing compared to the goings-on in the lobby. For some reason, the Philharmonia's directors were calling the scene on the stage a homosexual demonstration.

"Why did you bring those faggots here?" a despondent Gayoz asked. Their complaint was completely unexpected.

"Why faggots? They're normal guys. That's just their stage show, a bit eccentric . . ."

"Normal guys?! One lies down on the stage, the other gets on top of him, the third joins in, too. They're degenerates, not musicians."

The next point in the indictment against Aquarium concerned the song 'Marina', which has these lines:

> 'Marina told me, that it's
> Clear to her, that
> She is beautiful, but
> Life is useless, and
> It's time for her to marry a Finn.'*

* In order to leave the country.

Grebenschikov decided that the last line was a bit too bold, so instead of 'to marry a Finn' (Finna) he sang, 'To marry Eno' (Ena), which preserved the cadence and rhyme. But the judges, naturally, didn't know who Brian Eno was, and to them it sounded like 'to marry her son' (sina), which, naturally, was taken as another manifestation of sexual perversion. At first the organisers wanted to expel Aquarium from the festival on the spot, but they softened after lengthy 'clarifications' by Boris and myself. The group even played a second concert, in the town of Gori in a spacious, freezing circus hall located 100 metres from the birthplace of J. V. Stalin. This show was filmed by a Finnish TV crew and segments were included in their 40-minute film of the Tbilisi festival called 'Soviet Rock', which likewise included clips of Time Machine, Magnetic Band, Autograph, Integral and a jazz rock group from Turkmenista called Gunesh.

The real problems began for Aquarium on their return to Leningrad, where their rivals in the local rock mafia had already rushed to brief leaders of the city's cultural establishment on the Tbilisi epic, suitably embellishing the details . . . after which Aquarium lost its rehearsal space and Grebenschikov his laboratory job. The legend began to grow.

It should be noted that the new wave groups were not the only outsiders at Tbilisi-80; there were also the esteemed and conservative VIA bands from the opposite wing. VIA-75 (number one in Georgia), Ariel and the Stas Namin Group (formerly Flowers) came to the festival expecting an easy conquest and general adoration. Instead, they were received coolly by the public and, even more unexpectedly, failed to transport the judging committee into ecstasy. The announcement of the results of the competition was a genuine shock for them, and during the follow-up concert for the prize winners, Stas Namin, usually very visible and self-confident, stood humbly on the sidelines, watching from the wings, intently observing Autograph and all the others . . . realising he was looking at 'this year's model'.

(The ambitious Stas decided to take revenge for his defeat at Tbilisi by exploiting the traditional rivalry between Georgia and Armenia. In the summer of 1981 an outdoor pop festival was organised on his initiative in Yerevan, capital of Armenia. On the eve of the festival, rumours circulated that Paul McCartney and The Bee Gees would arrive. In fact, the headliners were Stas Namin, Magnetic Band, mainstream pop performers Valeri Leontiev and Jolly Kids plus a pair of jazz groups.)

The Tbilisi festival was not continued. Gayoz Kandelaki now heads the Caucasus department of Melodia and runs a bi-annual international jazz festival, the next of which will take place in September of 1988.

Tbilisi-80 brought the triumph of rock centrism—yesterday's establishment became today's dinosaurs and yesterday's underground became today's hits. Of course the same thing would have transpired had the festival never occurred, only a bit later and without such dramatic clarity. As it was, newspapers and radio began proclaiming the appearance of 'new talent' representing 'promising directions in young people's music'. Of course the fanfare was a bit late, but that made it no less deserved. The first era of rock on an official foundation had begun.

Andrey Makarevich had every reason to be happy, as might any man who spent 12 years digging a tunnel and had at last broken through into the light. He didn't seem to be basking in sunshine, though, during our only serious conversation at the festival, which took place on the eve of departing Tbilisi.

"So now you consider us a bourgeois sellout," Makarevich said, having in mind the post-festival press conference at which I had asserted that Time Machine now had every chance to become recognised pop stars, replacing boring, over-the-hill groups like The Gems, Pesnyari and others. "You think that if the judges have endorsed us and the Philharmonia has invited us to play, that means we've changed and we're not worth paying attention to. That's a very narrow point of view. Musicians, including rockers, need to work professionally, to earn money for their music. And you know that I haven't made any compromises for the sake of popularity, that we sing and play what's really important to us. We haven't become any worse or any dumber, it's just that attitudes towards the genre have changed, and towards us, too."

"I agree, but look at poor Aquarium—they were almost run out of town . . ."

"But doesn't it seem to you that's precisely what they wanted? To create a scandal, to make as abrasive an impression as possible, like it's done in punk rock. Incidentally, one needs to possess certain skills for that too. I don't believe that 'professionalism' is just playing technique. Professionalism is the ability to achieve one's desired results. Boris wanted to create an uproar, and he managed it well. Good for him! But we have never needed that kind of fame; I've never sought to shock anyone, although some may have perceived us as somehow threatening through their own stupidity. All of my songs in the end are about goodness, purity . . . love, if you wish. And thank god people have finally understood that and stopped talking rubbish about 'pessimism' and some 'hidden negative meaning'."

What could I answer? Yes, everything was in good order, of course. Time Machine had finally blossomed out from under the pavement and it would have been silly indeed to talk of stamping them back down. It's just that now there were other people, like Aquarium, who needed my support more.

This little clarification of relations with Andrey Makarevich soon found expression in a Time Machine song called 'Barrier'.

> 'You were enticed by every ban,
> You charged like a bull through every red light,
> And no one could turn you from your path,
> But if all the paths are opened,

Where to go, and with whom?
How would you find your way then?'

Yes, many paths were in fact suddenly opened. Complimentary articles about native rock appeared in the press. I had written my first article on Time Machine in 1976. It wasn't published, but in the spring of 1980 two were printed simultaneously. There had been occasional articles before, but they portrayed rockers mainly as anti-heroes, as under-cultured youth under a bad influence. The radio now began broadcasting songs that had previously been unacceptable. In Moscow's Komsomol Theatre and several others, rock musicals were staged with phenomenal success (the most famous of which was Alexey Rybnikov's 'Juno And Avos'). Most important of all, Time Machine, Autograph, Arax, Dialogue and Magnetic Band began triumphant concert tours of the sports arenas in major cities. On the street there appeared real advertisements with the words ROCK GROUP in big letters.

Rock's breakthrough to the big stage had a lot to do with commercial factors. Despite intensive cheerleading for VIA over TV and radio, the mass audience was pretty much sick of it and thus it no longer generated a reliable revenue. Concert organisations were losing money and underfulfilling their plans. Young people were waiting for rock and were ready to accept it; a decade of enraptured listening to foreign records and pilgrimages to unauthorised concerts had created all the preconditions. For all practical purposes, despite the total absence of support from governmental cultural organisations, rock had become the favourite music of millions of people, had become the norm. Now this 'norm' was assuming 'normal' forms. Listeners were waiting for a powerful sound with rhythm and drive and understandable Russian lyrics not limited to insipid banalities. And this is what they got.

Time Machine were the undisputed number one act. The hullabaloo around their first shows in Leningrad could almost be compared with the mass hysteria of Beatlemania. Thousands of teenagers descended upon the Jubilee Sports Palace; buses carrying the musicians executed complicated manoeuvres of deception to save Makarevich, Kutikov, Yefremov and Podgorodetsky from the ecstatic crowd. In Minsk, fans without tickets crashed the concert by breaking down doors. There were analogous happenings in almost every city the group visited. Of course, many were bothered by all this. After Time Machine's tour of Siberia, the newspaper *Komsomolskaya Pravda* published an open letter from local cultural activists with a harsh condemnation of the group, including the familiar accusation of 'not fitting our ideals' plus a call to repudiate the new 'false idols'. In answer, however, the editors received 250,000 (!) angry letters, many with 100 or more signatures, and the paper had no choice but to offer a tribune to the 'voice of the people' as it defended its heroes against the conservatives.

The ice broke in the record industry, too. Our rock discography begins (I have in mind LP records; various singles and flexidiscs had come out earlier) with an album by Apelsin, an Estonian group that played country rock, rockabilly and musical parodies. After that came the first significant record of Alexander Gradsky, called 'Russian Songs'. It was a remarkably striking and forceful interpretation of eight authentic folk songs spanning a thousand years of musical style, from pagan rituals to revolutionary marches. This music had nothing in common with the syrupy folk pop of Pesnyari or Ariel. Gradsky's songs were full of emotion, with original arrangements that conveyed a feel of historical retrospective. It was interesting music, in places even a bit terrifying.

One song, 'Cry', is absolutely fantastical and unlike anything I've ever heard. Gradsky mixed 10 vocal tracks where he sang as men, girls and hysterical old women wailing at an ancient funeral ceremony. Gradsky has a magnificent voice (he once had an audition at the Bolshoi Theatre), but swears that after recording this song he couldn't speak for a week. If this isn't rock, it's something even heavier. Of Gradsky's five albums, 'Russian Songs' remains unsurpassed. Most likely it's the uniqueness of the folklore that makes the difference, as Gradsky's own compositions are rather dull and even his remarkable singing doesn't save them.

The bestseller of the season, though, was not 'Russian Songs' nor even the latest disc from Alla Pugachova, but an album called 'Disco Alliance' by the previously unknown Latvian group Zodiak. The 10 electronic instrumental numbers on 'Disco Alliance' (which were strongly reminiscent of the then-popular French group Space) offered nothing noteworthy except the quality of the recording. Producer of the album was Alexander Griva, director of the Riga branch of Melodia, and he spared neither tape nor studio time on Zodiak, a group of young students from the conservatory (among whom was Griva's daughter, which may explain the producer's extra effort). The album that once caused such a sensation is now almost completely forgotten (and Zodiak broke up over four years ago), but 'Disco Alliance' left its mark by establishing certain norms for quality and by suggesting that it was not enough to play well and compose interesting songs, that one had to know how to work with sound as well. For some unknown reason Melodia never publishes figures on how many copies of its records are pressed, but informal calculations indicate that 'Disco Alliance' sold about five million copies, i.e. about the same number as the first Pesnyari LP or David Tukhmanov's albums.

The 1980 Olympic Games had no impact on Soviet rock. The cultural programme was jammed with our standard 'export' displays— folklore choruses and classical ballet and, of course, parades. I remember the Games only for the abundance of soft drinks from Finland, the funny English language announcements in the metro and the strangely empty streets and stores.* No, this was not like the Youth Festival of 1957 (as some had anticipated).

But one important event did occur at the end of July—Vladimir Vysotsky, the great Russian bard, died at the age of 43 of cirrhosis of the liver. Tens of thousands came to his funeral. One can say without any exaggeration that it was a truly national mourning—the force and magic of Vysotsky touched everyone, from school students to war veterans. His singing was an explosive mixture of pain, humour, sarcasm and desperate longing for truth. Moreover, as distinct from the abstract lyrics and artsy metaphors traditionally used by our 'singing poets', Vysotsky's best songs were full of all the real stuff of daily life and realistic, colourful characters. He didn't hide the dark and painful side of reality, and among the heroes of his songs were drunkards, thieves and derelicts. Judging by the heart-rending confessions he made in his songs (such as: 'Nothing is holy, not the church and not the *kabak**), it seems that Vysotsky himself lived partially on that dark and painful side.

Vysotsky was a professional actor at Moscow's Taganka Theatre (where he played, among other roles, a modern-day Hamlet with guitar), but his songs and the emotions expressed within them were so authentic that people identified him more with the characters in his songs, and Vysotsky grew into a genuine folk hero. Bureaucrats regarded him with apprehension, but couldn't ignore his universal popularity. Vysotsky was subject to the same hazy, duplicitous attitude as were the rock groups before 1980—no formal ban, but no official support. Only after his death were several records and a printed collection of his verses released, but that was only a drop in the ocean, as Vysotsky had written over 1000 songs.

Vladimir Vysotsky had no contact with the rock world (although he sang a bit like Beefheart or Tom Waits), and this sad fact was the fault of the rockers, who were naive and young and hadn't yet grown to the level where they could comprehend the world and its pain as portrayed by Vysotsky.

Also, most of those into rock were overly attracted to the music and didn't care about the words as much. Many had regarded singing in Russian as an unpleasant obligation, to be fulfilled with precision but no enthusiasm. By 1980 English was becoming old-fashioned and was losing its prestige (also advances in the quality of vocal amplifiers were exposing the weakness of our singers' English pronunciation). But the majority of Russian lyrics were so stylised and formal (and sometimes even ungrammatical) that Makarevich, for all his puritanical didacticism, remained the only thinking man's poet of the lot.

With the arrival of the new wave the situation began to change. Grebenschikov was the first purveyor of rough-edged lyrics. That same summer he brought me a cassette by a friend of his named 'Mike'. I

*During the Olympics, travel to Moscow by citizens from other Soviet cities was closed. Normally the daily flow of out-of-towners through Moscow numbers two million people.

* An old-style pub or café with a rowdy clientele and heavy drinking.

63

pushed the play button and heard the following (to a fast rock'n'roll rhythm but with acoustic guitar):

'I'm sitting on the toilet,
Reading Rolling Stone.
Venya's in the kitchen
Pouring out the samogon. *
Vera's asleep in the attic,
Though the tape player's screaming.
We should have woke her long ago,
But that would be "mauvais temps".

It's been raining for two days,
And I ought to get up but I'm lazy.
I feel like a smoke, but
I've got no cigarettes left.
I'm afraid of sleeping,
I guess I'm a coward.
All out of money,
With the outskirts blues.'

*Home-brewed liquor.

Boris' songs, which had just struck us for their street toughness, now seemed academic and stylised against this background. Our rock got an infusion of naturalism, of gutter realism. 'Outskirts Blues' became one of the anthems of the new music and simultaneously a bogeyman reviled by all champions of purity, including, incidentally, some rockers. On the cassette were other equally interesting songs, and Boris and I agreed that he would bring Mike to the capital at the first chance he got.

In the meantime, Moscow, rock Moscow, was deserted. Of the well known groups, only Sunday, formed by one Alexei Romanov, Makarevich's ex-sideman and imitator, remained outside the professional network and continued giving concerts in clubs outside Moscow (for which they were asking serious sums, as with any bogus goods). But there was absolutely nothing noteworthy about them, and the other acts around were even more boring (minor league groups like Mosaic, Rare Bird, Magic Twilight, and others). The progressive audience was enjoying shows by Last Chance, a skiffle band whose members played all sorts of children's and home-made instruments (besides acoustic guitar and violin) and put on a hilarious theatrical show with pantomime, athletic exercises and a spoof swindling of cash from the audience. The leader of Last Chance, Vladimir Schukin, wrote lovely melodies and sang with the touching voice of a wandering minstrel. For lyrics he used excellent verses from children's poetry—amusing and paradoxical, naive sounding but not at all dumb. My favourite was a song about a pedantic rat teaching a cat how to behave properly in public and in society; the cat hears him out and then eats him without comment.

In accordance with tradition, autumn meant it was time to organise something, but there was no question of a festival this time around since the new stars no longer needed one, while the bands of the new underground were still too few to fill one out. Thus one big concert was staged with Last Chance, Aquarium, A. Makarevich (solo), Kostya Nikolsky (co-leader of Sunday, also solo), Virgis Stakenas and Mike (real name Mikhail Naumenko). Aquarium by that time had entered a reggae phase and played without a single electric instrument; two thirds of the group had switched to percussion while Boris sat on a stool with his acoustic guitar. There were lots of good new songs: 'To Stand, I Have To Hold On To My Roots' (reminiscent of Tbilisi), 'Who Are You To Tell Me Who I Am?' (about 'reputable' people who took it upon themselves to judge the group), 'Counterdance' (a sad song dedicated to Makarevich, who had become reputable and lost his roots), 'My Friend The Musician' (could have applied to many, about how some rockers drink and blab more than they get anything done), and 'Someone Waits For Us Tonight' (a slightly paranoid number about bohemian life on the run).

Aquarium were well received, but the star of the evening was Mike. It was his first ever performance in a large hall. He came out in dark glasses and started off by recommending Havana Club rum and Leningrad's Belomor cigarettes to everyone. Then he sang 'Sweet N'.

'I woke up this morning in my clothes,
In an armchair in my closet in my own four walls.
I waited till dawn for you to come,
And I wonder, Sweet N., where you spent this night.

I washed and brushed my teeth,
Thought about it, but decided not to shave.
I stepped outside and followed my nose,
It was light outside and the day had begun.

And on the bridge I met a man
Who told me that he knew me.
He had a rouble and I had four,
And along those lines we purchased some wine.

And he took me to the strangest place,
Where everyone sat around a table with food
And drank port wine and played dice
And called each other shit.

It was a typical attic scene,
From two speakers wafted J. S. Bach,

65

> *Each thinking of his own affairs,*
> *One about 3 billion, the other about five roubles.*
>
> *And someone as always was blabbing about flying saucers*
> *And someone as always was preaching about zen,*
> *But I sat like a statue and wondered stupidly*
> *Where you spent this night, Sweet N.'*

That's about half the song, but I don't begrudge Mike a long quotation because his lyrics have a definite informative value, giving as they do a realistic portrayal of the lifestyle and spirit of Leningrad's 'attic' life.

One could have safely predicted that Mike would give the audience a real surprise, but the force and spontaneity of the reaction exceeded all expectations. When he sang his crowning number, 'You're Trash', part of the audience shouted 'bravo' and applauded while part booed and whistled after almost every line. (A tape of the show remains.) It was unreal, especially since this was not a crowd of effusive Georgians, but an over-civilised, snobbish crowd of capital youth.

So what was it about Mike that set them off so? Take any verse from 'You're Trash'—they're all about the same, describing the amoral lifestyle of the song's heroine and the author's tortured relations with her:

> *'You're sleeping with my bass player*
> *And playing bridge with his wife.*
> *I'll forgive him everything,*
> *But what to do with you?*
> *Ah, but I gave up on that long ago—*
> *Forward, my little one, go ahead.*
> *You're trash!'*

Nothing special, right? Nothing lofty, nothing terrible. All the same, for some it was a breakthrough in candour, while for others it was a deathly shock. And all for the simple reason that here, singing about such things was just not done, not accepted. In rendering various late night conversations and drunken confessions in rhyme, by putting forth today's unembellished rock hobo as the hero of his songs, Mike opened up a new aesthetic, a street aesthetic. He held up a mirror for everyone aimed, for the first time, right between the eyes.

> *'The bathroom is a place*
> *Where you can strip completely naked*
> *And toss away your smile, your fear*
> *And your honour along with your clothes.*
> *The mirror is your best friend—*
> *It'll spit right in your eye.*

But the bath water will take you as you are.'
(from 'Ode To The Bathroom')

It's worth noting that this aesthetic is closer to Vysotsky's than to Makarevich's. (Of course Mike didn't invent it himself; being a literate rock fan, he had, like Grebenschikov, translated texts by Bowie, Dylan, Bolan, Reed, Zappa and others for years.)

The other factor of Mike's effect on the audience was this: being innocent as a virgin when it came to the canons of official culture, he had inadvertently touched the Big Taboo, the skeleton in the closet of our rock music and, in fact, all our art—sex. Not by a long shot did he call everything by its name, but up to that point even such semicandour had been present only in a certain genre of uncensored songs associated with the denizens of the underworld.

So then, what shouldn't one sing about? What *needed* to be sung about? Advocates and opponents of Mike scuffled in the street after the concert, although only yesterday they hadn't known of their dispute or its provoker. Progressive writers, dramatists and directors walked about with dazed expressions, repeating over and over, an incantation, 'very interesting, very interesting', or 'simply amazing'. Mike was the most amazed of all; his debut had turned out something like Elvis Presley's first appearance on television. Two days later he wrote a song about it with the words 'Too many compliments, like empty flattery; hey Boris, what are we doing here?'

I'd never seen Makarevich as upset as he was after Mike's performance. "How'd you like it?" I asked. "I loathed it. I consider it vandalism." There was nothing I could answer. I realised that something was departing into the past for ever.

'On Saturdays I go to the Rock Club
They've got loads of great bands there
I enter proudly with a ticket in my hand
And they sing me songs in my native tongue.'
—'A Simple Guy's Song' by Mike And The Zoo Park.

IT WAS FEBRUARY 1981. I had two weeks of last year's vacation left over and I had to use them. Boris Grebenschikov and I flew to Tbilisi, where Boris has been promised excellent arrangements for some solo concerts. Instead we were lead aimlessly about town by a diminutive local girl to eat *khachapuri* (a cheese pie, Gruzia's answer to pizza) in cheap cafes. Thoroughly disappointed, Aquarium's leader left for Yerevan while I stayed in Tbilisi awaiting the arrival of Time Machine. We went together to a UEFA football match between Dynamo Tbilisi and West Ham. Somehow we were taken for English fans, but treated very cordially, of course. The next day we travelled to the mountains, to Bakuriani where Time Machine began downhill skiing lessons and I didn't know what to do with myself.

Makarevich was absorbed in his first cinema project, a film called *Soul* (in which Time Machine appeared as a nameless back-up band for two well-known pop stars, Sofia Rotaru and Mikhail Boyarsky. The film turned out badly; the whole exercise could only be justified by the presence of a few Time Machine songs. Makarevich even lost his royalty payment when it was stolen from his apartment). Life on the set of *Soul* revolved around personal intrigues (Alla Pugachova, who was to play the lead, had just divorced the film's director; who could replace her?) and talk of skis and ski boots. More stimulating was the company of Manana Menabde, an excellent singer of cruel romances and jazz ballads in decadent cabaret style who was living in the neighbouring hotel.

Several days later I left for Leningrad, as I had been invited to the birthday party of a certain Swine. My acquaintance with Swine (real name Andrey Panov) was the final event of my event-filled 1980. He had appeared without warning at our apartment one night in December around midnight. He was dressed like a character from a Sex Pistols poster, except that his outfit was a Russian-winterized version. I remember a mass of safety pins and a loud tie hanging out of a grimy coat. He said he was a punk (that much was evident) and produced for inspection a reel of tape wrapped in cellophane. "This is our bullet," he said. To be more precise, it was an apartment concert tape of the group Automatic Satisfiers, in which Swine was vocalist and songwriter. Again the mid-tempo, heavy fuzzbox guitar sound, plus a vocal fighting its way through an over-abundance of saliva in the oral cavity. Their keynote number went like this:

> 'Punks have appeared in Leningrad,
> Don't know whether they're people or monsters,
> They dance the twist and the pogo,
> Show us the road to Rotten!'

Other memorable lines:

> 'I took a walk to the junk yard
> And there I found a can.
> Black black caviar!
> Black caviar, expensive . . .'

After Grebenschikov and Mike this sounded like juvenile nonsense. I like naive stuff, but here the naivety was forced. What's black caviar got to do with anything?

Some of the songs were ravingly absurd, and they came off more humorous and even more authentic sounding:

> 'I came home.
> While the soup was still cooking
> My neighbour through the wall
> Shot himself with a gun.'

Like other Soviet 'punks', Swine had no ties to the working class and hardly qualified as a street kid—his father was a choreographer, his mother a ballerina. He had grown up, in his own words, "surrounded by half-naked women". I liked him more than his songs; he was an odd figure, not without a certain twisted charm and not too bad a singer. After hearing my critique of his tape Swine said that his music was a hundred times heavier 'live' and that I had to come to one of their concerts. Thus came about my invitation to his birthday celebration, which promised to be a punk rock happening.

The party took place in a dingy restaurant called The Bow or The Stern or something like that. The entire Leningrad punk commonwealth was in attendance, about 20 citizens plus an equal number of curious fellow travellers. The Automatic Satisfiers quickly proved that they couldn't play at all. What's worse, they were equally short on energy. Their sluggish anarchy on stage made an incongruous combination with the aggressiveness they showed toward the audience by spitting from all sides and smashing any and all tableware at hand. Swine was an able and improvising showman (from the School Of Utter Repulsiveness). And while his image was convincing, it was also uninteresting.

"OK, listen to your idols, The Sex Pistols," I began. "They're not just drunken, decrepit misfits. They play intense music and have enormous energy. They're nihilists, but they have something to say about social questions; and they don't come on as clinical idiots."

All attempts to shake up Swine, however, were in vain. He was genuinely indifferent to all of that and didn't try to pretend otherwise. "Yeah, that's what I am, a useless piece of crap . . . So what?" Such was his universal answer to all complaints. Mike (the only non-punk respected by the 'decrepit' crowd) captured this stoic debility at the core of Swine's character in a song dedicated to him called 'I Don't Know What I'm Living For, So To Hell With It'.

Since then I've seen Swine a few times. He continues singing the same songs, moreover he gets worse at it as the years go by. But since no other shining new talents of the genre have appeared, he remains the main, if not only, replica of Russian quasi-punk. And he has managed to generate a legend. Though few have met Swine, everyone has heard about the time he displayed his member during a performance . . . which is entirely plausible given that such concerts were held mainly in apartments or studios. The last time I saw Swine was in November 1986. He had grown very thin and told me that he wanted to go legal and join the Rock club. He was dressed in dirty white pants, a sailor's shirt and navy pea-jacket.

But back to the birthday party. The restaurant's manager, properly appalled by such a rowdy crowd, hurried to close up, and so the happening continued in a brightly lit café somewhere nearby. It was crowded there, so at first the Automatic Satisfiers and company had to be satisfied dancing the twist and pogo with middle-aged women they'd never met . . . which was considerably more jolly than their pathetic stage show.

Then the house orchestra abandoned stage and the 'acousticals' began—Mike followed by a couple of young singers. Viktor Tsoy from the group Ward Six sang the first (and at that time only) song composed by him, entitled 'My Friends March Through Life, The Only Stops Are At Beer Halls': 18 years old, horrible diction, Korean features, and an excellent, touching song about the aimless mood of some city teenagers. Next up was Alexey Rybin, a pale, emaciated first-year technical college student with one eye larger than the other who sang fast, one-minute songs.

'I don't want to be a laureate
*I don't want to live in the Astoria**
I don't give a damn that I'll never
Drink champagne in a deluxe suite.'

After that he sang 'Beasts', one of the strongest songs in Soviet rock. It's surprising, but unlike Tsoy, Rybin has written practically nothing since that time. But his first effort became a classic:

'Set up the glasses and pour,
What's next, you'll see for yourself,
And don't ask me questions, just know this,
That people are like beasts!
We're all like beasts in the dark forest.'

'Your bones are sharp, my teeth are whole,
It won't be easy to tear us to pieces.
Though we're beasts, we're no worse than others
Who are cruel like beasts!
Strong, like beasts in the wild forest.'

It wasn't the lyrics that were so powerful, but the way the melody built up to almost catapult the word 'beasts' out at the end of each verse so that everyone present sang it out, too. If one were to conduct a poll now on the topic: "Which Soviet rock song would you choose as an anthem?", I think the majority would choose Aquarium's tune 'Rock'n'Roll Is Dead (But I'm Not Yet)'. I'd choose 'Beasts' by the obscure Rybin, despite the unflattering allegory.

The next morning Boris Grebenschikov (in whose flat I was staying) handed me two documents to read entitled 'Proposal For A Rock Club' and 'Charter Of The Rock Club'. There, in the most official language imaginable I read a point-by-point outline of goals and tasks, rights and obligations, privileges and violations, hierarchy and functions for the newly-proposed organisation. The word 'rock' appeared infrequently and seemed preposterous in such a context. Take this phrase, for instance: "The rock club sets itself the goal of attracting youth to a wide range of amateur creative activities, of raising the cultural level of visual presentation and ideological artistic content in such performances, and likewise of portraying and propagandizing the best examples of national and international music in the given genre." These documents indicated that yet another attempt (the sixth to date) was being made in Leningrad to form an official organisation for the unofficial groups.

A couple of years later the president of the rock club, Nikolai Mik-hailov, would explain the motives in this way: "At the beginning of 1981 the number of concerts in the city had sharply decreased, since

71

the groups had no permission for official performances, while the city administration had become fairly effective at restraining the informal sessions. But there were over 50 known bands in Leningrad and a colossal, unfulfilled craving for concerts and socialising. Also, the authorities' attitude towards rock seemed to have softened after the Tbilisi festival. So the musicians and concert organisers bombarded the municipal organisations with requests to resolve the problem. And in the end we got a helping hand from the Centre For Individual Amateur Performance (DST by its Russian initials, an organisation that coordinated all types of amateur artistic activity—music, theatre, film making, dance etc.—on behalf of the trade unions). At that time the DST had just undergone a major change of personnel, including the appointment of a new director, and the new management was almost all women. They joked with us that if they lost their jobs because of us, at least their husbands could feed them."

I think that the city authorities made a conscious and intelligent compromise, because controlling the situation was truly problematic (as Swine's recent birthday party illustrated). But on the morning in question at Boris' flat I chuckled for a long time and made smug comments about the charter's bureaucratic clauses, as if the whole thing were a joke. It turned out that in this instance my intuition betrayed me completely. Or maybe I just underestimated the strength and cohesion of Leningrad's rockers in judging things from my Moscow point of view.

On the whole, Leningrad and Moscow are two completely different cities, both in appearance and spirit. I can't bear Leningrad's physical aspect—beautiful like a theatre set, but flat and straight like a chessboard. The only relief from its flatness are the arcs of its bridges, and the only violation of its geometric straightness are the twists of its rivers and canals. St Petersburg was built on an empty spot, among swamps, and that tension in the city's artificiality seems to press down on people to this day. One can be enraptured with Leningrad's architecture while simultaneously going crazy from claustrophobia. And it seems that all this somehow stimulates the creative process (recall Gogol and Dostoevsky).

Leningrad is a more Western city than Moscow. The presence of the port and the abundance of foreign tourists (especially Scandinavians, who come by the thousands at weekends) has not only created an enormous parasitic industry of *fartsovschiki*, but also facilitated more effective penetration of foreign ideas and trends among youth. (*Fartsovschiki* are a horde of individual entrepreneurs, aged 10 to 40, who 'attack' foreigners on the street in broad daylight with demands to buy, sell or exchange things. They're a very dispiriting lot who make one ashamed. Strange that in the midst of all this action the militia seemed occupied only with keeping order at concerts.)

Leningrad is only half the size of Moscow, and despite its refinement is somehow provincial. Moscow is a gigantic crossroads, a sprawl of neighbourhoods and scenes with no connection between one another, a place where one can live for years and not know about what's going on around the corner. Leningrad is more unitary, everything there is in plain view. The end result is that in Leningrad a single artistic community of rock musicians and other bohemians developed. As in a big village, there are places in Leningrad where one can find everyone without any advance arrangements. The main such place for the young artistic community is a famous café on the corner of Nevsky and Liteiny known informally as Saigon. (There are many versions on the origin of the name; all date back to the sixties.) Each member of the in-crowd registers his presence there at least once a day, and from five to six in the evening one can find almost anyone who's anyone standing at one of the counters over a cup of coffee and learn all the news and gossip in the city. For me this was curious, for Leningraders it was sacred. The Saigon figures in countless rock songs; one group even has a tune called 'We Are The Children Of Saigon'. Many feel that on that corner there's some special kind of energy.

And so the children of Saigon united in a rock club, and the debut concert took place on March 7. The main groups in Leningrad at that time were the Rossiyanye,* The Myths and Picnic. The latter two were almost identical—they played hard rock and blues and sang lyrics that reminded one strongly of Makarevich. All the standard signatures of the seventies came through in their music, although Yuri Ilchenko had stopped playing long before. (At present both are professional and sound a bit more modern; The Myths remind me of Dire Straits, Picnic of Howard Jones.)

The Rossiyanye were without question original and charming in their own way, and provoked serious disagreement among fans and experts. If one can imagine something like a cross between free-wheeling drinking songs and heavy metal, such was their style. They had unkempt long hair and a completely reckless stage manner; they expended massive energy and drove audiences to hysteria. Their guitarist and singer Georgi Ordanovsky rarely performed sober and showed some spontaneous, acrobatic moves that Nils Lofgren and Springsteen would envy. Their bass player (nicknamed Sam) was missing three fingers on his right hand. An evening with the Rossiyanye was always boisterous and unpredictable. They might have made it as the perfect model of authentic Russian rock, except that they lacked the most elementary 'meaningfulness', and for this the intellectuals disdained them. Even Kolya Vasin, who was remote from snobbish aestheticism, considered them 'talented mediocrities'. Their lyrics were simplistic and the music seemed to consist of nothing but choruses. Naturally this didn't prevent them from being a genuinely popular group. After the rock club legalised the

*An archaic term for Russians.

Rossiyanye, their open-air summer concerts drew thousands, and the term 'Rossiyanomania' made the rounds.

The rock club's organisational structure was a three-tiered hierarchy. The base of the pyramid was the general membership, whose ranks included a few hundred musicians, plus artists, photographers, collectors, organisers and others. Once each year the members' general meeting elected a council, made up of seven of the more esteemed and active club members, headed by a president. The council members directed all the club's day-to-day work—auditioning new groups, searching out rehearsal spaces, organising concerts and seminars, maintaining contacts with the press, advertising the club's events and so forth. Finally, at the top of the pyramid were the club's 'curators'—officials of DST. They didn't interfere in the club's internal workings, but authorisation to hold concerts and approval of individual bands' participation depended on their say.

Concerts began in the spring of 1981 and were a great success, but this didn't mean that the rock club had solved all problems for everyone. For one thing, groups could not receive a fee for their performances; such was the official doctrine on 'amateurs' until the mid-eighties. Thus, the hopes of 'commercial' bands like The Argonauts and Stage Coach went unrealised, and they split off from the rock club, preferring the provincial but professional philharmonias. Secondly, the rock club had no equipment and no space of its very own. The DST hall at 13 Rubinstein Street had to be shared with a theatre group and other amateur cultural organisations, and these rather underprivileged conditions forced the rock club to walk the fine line between pure enthusiasm and the traditional machinations employed previously for arranging 'sessions'.

Thirdly, the liberalism of the club's curators didn't extend to the more extreme bands in town. Swine and company were left out, as was Bugle Call, a boring group (sort of like Uriah Heep with reverb overdose) that sang banal songs on evangelical themes and enjoyed special favour with the BBC and Voice Of America. The rock club explained its decision not to admit these groups on the grounds that they would not be able to give concerts. In Bugle Call's case, because religious propaganda is forbidden in 'secular' establishments—in their Baptist church they were allowed to play, and did so. (Some time later, around 1983, two members of Bugle Call were arrested and convicted for an unlawful attempt to cross the Soviet-Finnish border. I had no contact with Bugle Call—because their work, in my view, was utterly uninteresting—and so I don't know the details of their 'crusade'. But the result might not have been so sad if the rock club and city authorities had shown more flexibility, and if Bugle Call had concerned itself more with the local audience and less with generating scandalous publicity in the West.) As for the Automatic Satisfiers, the opinion of the rock club's council was that they simply couldn't play, and in fact many weak bands (not just 'punks') were denied a place in the rock club on the same grounds.

Besides the scandalising Rossiyanye, the rock club's 'left wing' was manned by Aquarium, and since they are one of the most significant (along with Time Machine) as well as unusual and influential groups in the history of Soviet rock, it's worth talking about them in more detail. Aquarium didn't present itself to the world as a rock group, but more as a kind of family or commune (their philosophy stemming partly from that of their beloved Grateful Dead) living in their own, isolated world. That's how they explain their name: you can see them (and they can see you), but they have their own separate environment. The Jerry Garcia role in Aquarium is played by Boris 'Bob' Grebenschikov—a somewhat mysterious but thoroughly friendly and peace-loving poet-singer-guitar player who spends most of his time at home over tea, reading fairy tale fantasy literature (Tolkein and others) and western music magazines. He's a fairly self-indulgent but democratic guru.

Vsevolod 'Seva' Gakkel (originally von Gakkel, as was recently discovered), descendant of one of the first Russian aviation designers, plays the cello and once upon a time graduated from music school. Seva is one of the brightest and most irreproachable individuals I know—calm, disarmingly unselfish, with a gleam in his eyes and the smile of a saint. He usually plays softly, providing a harmonic background for Aquarium, but I have one tape from a raucous Moscow concert during the hot summer of 1981 when Gakkel played such a soul-piercing solo that I get chills just recalling it. And it was on one of Aquarium's most enduring songs, 'The Good Dilettante':

> 'She's afraid of fire, you're afraid of walls.
> Shadows in the corners, wine on the table,
> Listen, do you remember why you're here?
> Who are you waiting for here?
> She cries at night, you can't help,
> After each day comes a new night.
> Here you met those more unhappy than you.
> Is that who you waited for?
> We know a new dance, but we have no legs,
> We went to a new film, but someone cut off the power.
> The Good Dilettante is on his way to the grocery.
> Is that what you waited for?
> I didn't know it was my fault,
> I just wanted to be loved.
> I just wanted to be loved!'

Whereupon begins the nerve grinding cello solo . . .

Andrey 'Dyusha' Romanov (no relation) plays flute and sings back-up vocals. A generous, sociable guy who likes a drink and a chat—especially a chat about Aquarium. It was to none other than Dyusha that Boris dedicated his song 'My Friend The Musician', which ends with the words 'To the glory of music, we'll begin today with cognac'. Dyusha is the most touching, helpless and, in a certain sense, the most 'Russian' component in Aquarium (despite his ever present Jethro Tull t-shirt). As to his background and education (probably college level) I have no idea, although we've been friends for years.

Finally there's Mikhail Vasilyev—bass player, percussionist and Aquarium's main channel of communication with the outside world. He's a computer programmer and the only one in the band with a career outside of Aquarium. (The others all work as janitors, night watchmen and the like, so as to have more free time.) He also performs all the administrative and financial functions for the band, though not very effectively if one takes into account the fact that from 1972 (when the group began playing together) until the present they haven't managed to save enough money to buy equipment and instruments. Mikhail likes to portray himself as a realist, a pragmatist if you will (he's a member of the rock club's council), but in fact he's the same kind of harmless lag as the rest of the band.

That's the basic foursome; various guitarists, drummers and a bassoon player have joined them at one time or another.

In Leningrad Aquarium were not popular. In the late seventies they played several times as support for Time Machine and, in the words of Kolya Vasin, "the audience suffered in agony, wondering when the boring, pretentious crap would finally cease." (Up until their 'punk' phase of 1979–80 Aquarium played meditative folk rock with countless esoteric influences.) Fame and glory came to them in Moscow, but on the banks of the Neva they began to score points only in 1982 when electric guitarist Alexander Lyapin and drummer Piotr Troschenkov were recruited. Lyapin was a virtuoso blues guitarist who had been in professional bands and had played jazz but wound up disenchanted and came to Aquarium seeking an outlet for his extraordinary and highly emotional style of playing. (If not in his sound, then at least in his feel and loose mannerisms he was closer to Jimi Hendrix than any other Soviet rock guitarist.) Lyapin injected into Aquarium that which it had never had before—a powerful rock sound and tight, technically proficient playing. But his relationship with the group was complicated and even traumatic. On the one hand, Boris needed him as a bridge to the rock audience, while on the other he envied Lyapin for the riveting solos and awesome stunts he performed in concert (playing with his teeth and behind his back, etc.) which shunted the leader into the shadows and won laurels for Lyapin. In addition, Lyapin was 'just a musician' and among Aquarium's artful mystics came off as something of a simpleton who didn't fit their otherworldly image. At times Lyapin would take offence at the supercilious attitude displayed towards him, but he was basically a jovial man and easily appeased and so he just kept on playing. And in time he became for all practical purposes the second most popular member of Aquarium, despite his actual status as a hired hand. As for the drummer Piotr, he was much younger than the rest, played reliably and behaved modestly. In evenings when there were no concerts he would play in restaurant bands.

With the arrival of these two new players Aquarium took a sharp turn from acoustic reggae and folk ballads towards mainstream rock, with episodic excursions into ska and funk. The culmination of their new electrified programme were two songs written under the obvious influence of The Doors—'Rock'n'Roll Is Dead (But I'm Not Yet)' and 'We'll Never Grow Older'. The latter (imagine something like a cross between 'When The Music's Over', and 'Decades' by Joy Division) contained these lines:

> *'I didn't know it was all so simple,*
> *I've even grown to a new height,*
> *But in these rivers there's water*
> *That I drink up without waiting for a toast.*
> *We drank that pure water,*
> *We drank that pure water*
> *And we'll never grow older.'*

From other bands this might have been mere sloganeering, pretty but empty. From Aquarium it was genuine. Noble naivety was their trademark—for its sake Aquarium have suffered, but thanks to it Aquarium have won victories. They may have seemed somewhat infantile, feeble and unfinished, but at the same time they had made no compromises and hadn't sold out. The pure water of rock idealism had cleansed Aquarium in a fundamental way. Sometimes they bored and even aggravated me—one wanted actions in place of preaching, broken glass instead of crystal. But then I would find myself sitting around the table with them again and see those transparent, childlike expressions through the cigarette smoke and all my anger would disappear. After all, who of us over 30 didn't drink that pure water?

I should add that Mike Naumenko also played with Aquarium for a bit, contributing his jagged guitar solos to their sound. After his triumph in Moscow Mike's life couldn't remain the same, and in early 1981 the group Zoo appeared. The manner in which it was formed corresponded perfectly to Mike's peculiar nature, which is impractical and basically lazy. So, to get himself a group he predictably took the easiest course of action available—rather than pick and choose musicians to get something worthwhile, he casually engaged a dreadful pick-up band called Black September, renamed them and became their leader. Their playing ability wasn't up to the standard of even his garage level rhythm'n'blues, but the irresistable irony of his lyrics and his spicy themes somehow compensated.

Membership in the rock club exercised little influence on Mike's cheeky songwriting. One of the big hits of the season, for instance, was a song written to a girl he met in the Saigon, whose 'eyes said "Yes!" to my greedy gaze', whereupon the two hopped on her bike and sped away together (passing a Lada and running red lights along the way). Face to face in her flat, the author asserts: 'I was innocent as a child and modest as a monk, until that night when I saw in your eyes . . . *strakh!*' (which means fear, except that Mike dropped the initial 's' and pronounced *trakh,* which is slang for sex).

But his real show stopper was an epic, 20-minute piece with 15 verses and more than 50 characters called 'In The Rural Town Of N . . .' The town is populated with historical luminaries and literary heroes— Galileo the disc jockey puts on a record and exclaims: "It spins after all!"; Romeo sees Juliet home from the cinema and then hurries off to a brothel; Oscar Wilde is in charge of the vice squad, while Mayakovsky* sells carrots at the market . . . Raskolnikov* makes his living sharpening axes and scissors on the street; Beethoven, the ex-king of rock'n'roll, plays nights in a bar on a broken down piano, while Anna Karenina languishes at a railroad station where no trains arrive. This righteous attempt at such sweeping iconoclasm (incidentally, the song also makes mention of the Jesus Christ & Father trading company) is amusing in some spots, banal in others. Nonetheless, a single mention of the familiar figures (especially controversial ones like Chairman Mao or famous pop singers) elicited a stormy reaction.

The Zoo's first big concert took place, as one might have guessed, in Moscow. We managed to convince the manager and crew of Time Machine to lend their equipment. It was kept secret from their leader but somehow he turned up for the show . . . and you can imagine Makarevich's joy at suddenly seeing Mike singing into *his* microphone. In fact, the antagonism between these two influential rockers found expression in Mike's song 'In The Rural Town Of N . . .,' where he sings: 'That's our youth hero, he organised a fight with some idiots, but he's fighting with himself.' This, of course, was aimed at a famous Time Machine song and its author. To Makarevich's credit, he didn't respond to this nasty attack.

New wave gained momentum slowly but surely. In 1982 two interesting new groups appeared—Kino and Strange Games. Kino was a duo consisting of two figures already familiar to us, Viktor Tsoy (vocals and rhythm guitar) and Alexey Rybin (lead guitar). Tsoy wrote all their songs, the dominant mood of which was solitude and an incessant thirst for contact and love:

*Celebrated Russian constructivist artist from the twenties and thirties.
*The murderous protagonist from Dostoyevsky's Crime and Punishment, set in Leningrad.

78

'It's raining since morning, and my pocket is empty,
My watch shows six, I've no fags and no fire.
In the familiar window there is no light.
I have time, but no money, and no one to visit.'

Like Mike, Tsoy sang of everyday city life, but from a completely
different point of view. Mike had no illusions and a healthy cynicism.
It was the view of a mature person—he has problems, but he knows
their limits and is capable of toying with them in song. Tsoy was still
a teenager only yesterday and at heart remained one still. His world is
sincere, full of confusion and rather defenceless. He wants to be grown-
up and sarcastic, but reality continues to surprise him:

'Spring—don't have to warm my beer,
Spring—soon the grass will grow,
Spring—just look how beautiful it is,
Spring—I've lost my head.'

While at the same time:

'I don't know how to sing about love,
I don't know how to sing about flowers,
And if I sing, it means I lie,
I don't believe it's all like that!
Through the wall the TV screams,
Another year has gone so fast,
Last year I sat here the same way,
Alone, alone, alone,
Searching for ideas for a new song.'

Boris Grebenschikov became Tsoy's main fan and benefactor, saying
that no one's songs had so much tenderness and purity. Which was
probably right. Excellent melodies too.

Strange Games immediately made a big splash and won a mass of
followers. It was a striking, impressive band, and the first of its kind.
Whereas the other acts performing new rock, from Aquarium to Automatic Satisfiers, concentrated on lyrics and didn't bother themselves
much with the rest, Strange Games were the first to get serious about
arrangements and a stage show. They played real ska and, to be honest,
borrowed a lot from Madness, both musically and visually. (They even
came out on stage in the same 'caterpillar' walk as shown on the cover
of the first Madness LP.) But one would hardly call them plagiarists—
their melodies had a palpable ethnic feel, as did their hilarious stage
moves. Their usual encore number went like this: Grigory Sologub
(guitar) would array himself in the garb of a village elder (fur hat, felt

boots and all), pick up an accordion, furrow his brow earnestly, and break into 'Smoke On The Water', after which the rest of the band kicked in and the hard rock anthem turned into a folk dance number. (In this way Strange Games avenged Madness' version of Swan Lake.)

Strange Games contained a mix of very distinct individuals, each a strong figure in his own right. Their leader Alexander Davydov (who died in 1984 after leaving the group) was a mysterious melancholic, while the Sologub brothers Grisha and Vitya (who played guitar and bass) were punkishly aggressive; keyboard man Kolya Gusev had a bright mind and biting manner, saxophone player Alexey Rakhov conjured up the old adorable stilyagi, and drummer Alexander Kondrashkin quickly earned a reputation as the best rock drummer in Leningrad. Unfortunately the abundance of personality couldn't help them when it came to writing strong lyrics, and so Strange Games used the verses of Western modernist poets (translated into Russian, of course). Vocals were another problem—almost everyone in the group sang, each in a distinct style but each equally middling. Strictly speaking there was no leader in Strange Games, or there were too many . . . which doomed them to a short lifespan. (The final break occurred in 1985.)

On stage, though, they were magnificent—comical, chaotic and impetuous. They elbowed each other away from the microphones, exchanged instruments, provoked the audience and otherwise clowned around, but the anarchy was exquisitely organised.

The rock club's first two years were marked by struggles between various factions, and searching for a means of existence. Consolidation of the situation came about in the spring of 1983, in preparing for the first Leningrad rock festival. More than 50 groups were filtered down to 14 of the best, who performed over the course of three sunny days in May on the rock club's stage at DST. It was not only a celebration, it was an act of self-affirmation. The festival was attended by journalists, art critics, 'official' composers, poets, rock activists and fans from different cities. From a rock reservation of dubious repute, the club changed in the twinkling of an eye into a cultural institution. Fortunately the transformation to reputability wasn't complete—the spirit of Saigon continued to circulate through the joyous crowd, and the officials in attendance scurried about with worried expressions for fear some scandal would occur.

In keeping with our unavoidable tradition, the festival was conducted as a competition. Of the good bands, we managed to give an award to everyone but Zoo, who played dreadfully. Third place was shared by Strange Games, Picnic, The Rossiyanye and Tambourine (easy melodic folk under the direction of Vladimir Levi, formerly of Flamingo and Last Chance). Second place went to The Myths and Aquarium. Winner of the grand prize was a new band called Manifaktura.

Other than the rock club council members, no one had even heard of Manifaktura before the festival, so their debut would have to be called more than a mere success. Driven by the keyboards of Oleg Skiba, the group played dreamy romantic songs (not without the influence of Ultravox) set in the typical Leningrad mood—a mixture of melancholy and nervousness. In fact their show was a theatricised 'theme' piece entitled 'The Waiting Room'. It opened with a railway station rush scene. Vocalist Viktor Saltykov began singing while lying on a bench, wrapped in his overcoat. Subsequently we find him hustling along Nevsky Prospekt and languishing in a turn-of-the-century sitting room.

At the close of the set he has perched himself on a ladder up near the ceiling of the hall, singing the song about a house he has built in the clouds. With their trendy 'new romantic' style, cute and completely safe lyrics plus their tender age, Manifaktura accommodated everyone and were proclaimed a 'great hope'. Unfortunately their first smash success proved to be their last—after the festival they gave several bland concerts (it seemed as if the first place prize had tripped them up psychologically) and that summer Skiba and guitarist Dmitri Matkovsky were called up for army service. Later they tried several times to reconstruct Manifaktura—like magicians trying to repeat a trick that had once worked—but without success. This group remains a rare example of a 'one hit wonder' in Soviet rock.

Along with Aquarium and The Rossiyanye, Manifaktura played a free festival in July in Vyborg, a city to the north of Leningrad near the Finnish border. It was not the most significant event of the season (in terms of the artistic level of the performances), but did qualify as the most spontaneous and enjoyable. The landscape was unforgettable —a suburban park called Monrepo on the beach of the Gulf of Finland, trees and boulders and the roar of the tide, a wooden stage 10 metres from the warm waves. The summer crowd occupied the large lawn plus the surrounding hills; those who so wished could listen to the music without leaving the water. The sun was shining. Several militiamen took in the scene and the songs in relaxed amazement.

> 'I'm hurrying home in a taxi,
> My wife is home with her lover.
> Our neighbour called me at work,
> She saw everything from her balcony.
> He arrived in a beige hat,
> Brought her flowers and a small cake.
> They met last summer in Anapa*
> While I was driving back and forth to the airport . . .
> Jealousy, jealousy!!'

*A Black Sea resort.

The song belonged to Moscow's Centre (more on them later), who were the only sober group at the concert. The Leningrad rock stars over-indulged themselves with the audience and played poorly. There had been festivals with larger crowds (the attendance at Vyborg was around five thousand) and ones with better sounds, but the unrestricted atmosphere and the casual lack of organisation were a first. The only analogous memory that comes to mind is of a festival in Vilyandi, Estonia, in the mid-seventies.

The Vilyandi festival had receded into the past like the crowds of hippies in home-made clothes. Estonia, however, had remained a centre of intense (though fairly isolated) rock culture. It was the only region where rock had always enjoyed full official support—and not just in terms of commercial exploitation. The mass media, including television, kept the republic's one and a half million citizens informed in detail about happenings in the genre. The local branch of Melodia, despite the bureaucratic red tape spun by the management in Moscow, had issued a steady stream of rock albums: the early eighties had seen the release of works by Magnetic Band, Ruya, Kaseke, Musique-Seif, Sven Grunberg and others. (Grunberg's exercise in electronic meditative music, entitled 'Breath', was highly regarded by the magazine *Eurorock*. 'Amazing that the musician managed to achieve such effects using such simple technology,' their review concluded.)

The Tallin cinema studio shot a film called *The Hit Of The Summer* in which all the top Estonian groups participated in one form or another. The Estonian Union Of Composers also displayed a sympathetic, supportive attitude toward the rockers and even collaborated with them a bit, offering their own more 'progressive' compositions for performance and helping with the organisation of concerts.

This attractive and nurturing atmosphere yielded the rather strange result that Estonian rock music gravitated towards two poles—pop bands playing pure entertainment music, and experimental groups playing jazz rock, sympho-rock, avant-garde and the like (all of which the Estonians christened 'prestigious rock'). The only trait common to both was a faultless mastery of playing technique. Incidentally, many musicians from the 'prestigious' clan would sign temporary contracts with the commercial groups and tour with them to earn a little extra cash. It would be no exaggeration to say that tiny Estonia gave Soviet rock as many talented musicians as Moscow and Leningrad together. The only disadvantage of this situation was that between the two poles there was a kind of vacuum: one didn't find the 'angry' socially concerned groups that were the strength of Russian rock . . . although there were a few brilliant exceptions.

The development of rock in Estonia is easiest to trace by following the Tartu festivals, which began in 1979 and became an annual display of the genre's latest achievements. Tartu is something along the lines of an Estonian Oxford—a small town with a large and celebrated university. Tartu has narrow cobblestone streets, ancient cottages, parks and hills, a quiet intellectual atmosphere, good beer—all in all a fantastically quaint spot. A small river flows through the centre of town and in early May, when it's not yet navigable, passenger boats are laid up along the banks. It's in these boats that musicians and their entourage usually live when they arrive for the festival. (Knowing what goes on aboard these boats at night, one can only be thankful that no one has fallen overboard.) The concerts are held at the largest building in town, a famous theatre called Vanemuine (The Old Mill). The organisation is first rate, and Russians who make it to Tartu walk around with their eyes wide open, silently envying the goings on—stage workers with walkie talkies, no militia visible, posters and badges with the festival emblem on sale, a press centre and late night bar on the premises. In the last few years the concerts have been filmed on video, and tapes are shown at night in the discotheque, interspersed with new music videos from the West . . . "You can't forbid someone to live well," as we Russians say. It's worth noting that all these wonders are performed by graduates, students and tutors of the university—in other words, by enthusiasts. If organisation was handled by official people, as usually happens, the picture wouldn't create such an impression.

Here are details of the main events at Tartu's festivals, year by year:

1980. The group In Spe (short for In Speranza, which means 'in the tone of hope') played Erkki-Sven Tüür's 'Symphony For Six Performers,' an engaging piece of 'medieval' rock that reminded me of Mike Oldfield's early compositions. The musicians' seriousness and spirituality was simply stunning. Erkki-Sven's father is a Baptist minister who lives on a small island. In Spe made their own start playing in a church, which didn't stop them, however, from becoming an acknowledged rock group and releasing two albums. In 1981 I invited them to Moscow, where they also had some success.

Propeller played an absolutely stunning set. It was real unrestrained punk rock. The band played fast, rough and tight, but the focus of attention was Peter Volkonsky. What a unique, remarkable character! He was a brilliant actor of the grotesque, an irresistable rough diamond of a singer and an uninhibited, introverted dancer . . . among other strong points. Cyrano de Bergerac had his unreal nose, but Peter's entire external aspect—his hands, his legs, his bearing, his walk, his voice— was distinguished by a special incongruity. Even on crowded streets in the centre of Tallin you couldn't fail to notice him from a distance, such a strange figure he cut. He had graduated from the philosophy department of Tartu University, directed a small experimental theatre studio and acted in movies, but his main 'occupation' was disturbing Estonia's placid artistic scene in any and every way possible with his mercurial temperament and unbridled fantasy, his explosive blend of genius and lunacy. Propeller was only one of his many projects—the most outrageous, but far from the most enduring. Several months after

Tartu-80 the group played one of Tallin's stadiums, and after the show some of the young concert-goers kicked up a bit of a ruckus. Propeller were asked to discontinue their performances. (Strange, though, that they don't ban football teams in similar situations.)

1981. Propeller minus Volkonsky had renamed itself Kaseke and won the grand prize for an instrumental programme. Peter made an appearance on the festival's final day wearing a Reagan mask and added to his terrible reputation. In Spe performed 'Lumen Et Cantus', a mass written in the Gregorian choral tradition. Ruya, idols of the seventies, marked the return to their ranks of pianist and composer Rein Rannap with a set of terse, powerful songs in standard punk riffs. 'Yesterday I Saw Estonia' was especially good.

Estonia's most popular band at the time, Rock Hotel, was in fact a supergroup of veterans from other bands—Heigo Mirka, the greying bass player previously of The Optimists, Margus Kappel, the stylish keyboard player from Ruya, and singer Ivo Linna, disenchanted from endless touring with Apelsin. Rock Hotel's repertoire was almost exclusively rock'n'roll classics from the fifties. They politely declined a place in the festival's official programme (by explaining, "We don't play original material") and instead played in the evening at dances.

1982. The grand prize went to Radar, a jazz rock band led by Paap Kylar, former drummer of Psycho. Live in concert Radar sounded exactly like Billy Cobham or George Duke on record. The funk group Mahavok was designated 'hope of the future'.

Among an abundance of country rock, pop and fusion, the only real discovery (for me, at least) was Kontor (Office). Dressed in deadly 9–5 office gear (some even in armlets), their show had a spirit of cabaret decadence and ranged in style from teary retro-swing to an Estonian version of Talking Heads' 'Psychokiller'. The tone was set by a gaunt frontman with bowler hat and cane, a professional actor, mime artist and magician named Heino Seljamaa. The overall stage manner was a kind of gloomy kitsch that contained a rather sharp satirical element in the opinion of many Estonians.

In a way it's harder for me to write about Estonian rock than about English or American, since the meaning of the lyrics always slips by me; it's not enough to get one or two key phrases translated by friends. And the fact that Estonian groups put less emphasis on words than do Russian groups is small consolation, especially at moments when the whole audience is laughing or applauding a certain phrase, and you sit there feeling like an alien. This particular problem became acute at the next festival.

1983. For the first time, Hardy Volmer's group, the most lively and problematic product of Estonian rock in the early eighties, was allowed to play at Tartu. The group was centred on inventive young intellectuals from Tallin's Academy Of Arts, and due to troublesome relations with some authorities the band's name had been changed several times. First it was called Fictitious Trust Co., then Turist. In Tartu the band introduced itself as Totu Kool, the Estonian rendition of a popular Soviet children's book whose hero is a small, unkempt rebel who always does the opposite of what he should. Hardy Volmer, the band's singer and guiding light, ran out on stage with a butterfly net and a tin drum on his chest. He beat his drum like Gunter Grass' well-known hero and sang with pure childish innocence about the absurdity and falsehood of the 'grown-up' world—about careerism, craving for material things, society gossip, the cult of money. The group played energetic, rough cut music (a bit like The Clash) which they dubbed neuro-rock, and the description was apt. A remarkable group! They had everything usually lacking in Estonia's sleepy, academic bands.

Heino Seljamaa's band couldn't make it to Tartu in full contingent, and so the public was presented with a vocal trio, Kontor-3. They came out in official-looking suits, briefcases in hand, and sang a perfect parody of the highly stylised music of the forties familiar to us from songs like 'March Of The Women's Brigades' or 'Hail To The Shock Workers'. It was a merciless act of grotesque. The chairman of the Tartu festival judges committee, the veteran popular music composer Valter Oyakäer, said to me sadly: "Of course, all that looks a bit ridiculous now, but why stir up the past like that? The singers who performed those songs are on in years now—how can you make fun of them in such a way?" Actually, I saw the point of the parody as something else, namely that 'bureaucratic pop' was not in fact a thing of the past (one need only take a look at any popular music show on TV to be convinced of that). Kontor-3 were only giving a pointed and timely reminder that lots of current popular music still bore a strong resemblance to its old, allegedly distant roots.

Peter Volkonsky returned. From the props of his theatre, which had once staged *The Physicists* by Durenmatt, he took costumes, masks and wigs, dressed up the musicians of In Spe and called them Archimedes, Pascall, Oppenheimer, Kurchatov and so forth; he called himself Einstein and the band $E = MC^2$. He had composed an anti-nuclear suite entitled 'Five Dances Of The Final Spring' (as if he had somehow sensed what would happen three years hence), and it was stunning.

The music was a hyper-emotional collage of rock, noise, classical music and avant-garde, and by virtue of his volcanic presence Volkonsky forced the musicians to play with unbelievable intensity. For his part, he not only sang but also recounted, with the audience and band in silence, the principles and types of nuclear reactions and the history of the creation of the atomic and hydrogen bombs. The finale, with the stage and the hall in total darkness, was a prolonged incantation, like a mantra: 'Listen to the light falling down'. Immediately after the concert I ran to the portable studio of Radio Estonia and asked: "Did you get $E = MC^2$ on tape?" They answered that they hadn't bothered, since they knew they wouldn't be able to use it for broadcast. The suite was subsequently performed once or twice more, but again without being recorded. It's tragic—one of the most impressive works of Soviet rock apparently disappeared without a trace.

At one of the evening jam sessions Heino Seljamaa and Peter Volkonsky danced a wild tango, and Peter got into such a frenzy that on one pirouette he broke his leg in front of the whole crowd, who were dying of laughter. The prize for 'hope of the future' again went to Mahavok, which indicated both the establishment's reluctance to recognise new music and a general stagnation in the scene. I became fully convinced of this at the next year's festival, when there was nothing at all worth hearing except for Hardy Volmer's Turist.

In neighbouring Latvia the general situation developed with more drama than in the comfortable confines of Estonia. Several prosperous collective farms emerged as the main patrons of the arts, offering the more well-known groups a rather interesting and unusual form of mutually beneficial collaboration. The collective farms purchased expensive equipment for the musicians and provided rehearsal space; the groups, for their part, toured under the aegis of their sponsoring collective farm, thereby bringing these progressive establishments both praise and profit.

In essence, the groups were semi-professional and offered appreciable competition to those performing in the state concert organisations. This type of collaboration proved so beneficial that several of the established professional bands transferred into the 'collective farm philharmonia' system, where they earned more money and enjoyed greater control over their work. Such was the case with Martin Brauns' group, Sipoli, whom I have already discussed. Their repertoire now consisted of two parts—simple pop songs for teenagers from provincial towns, and overblown theatrical numbers (including an adaptation of Kipling's *Mowgli*) aimed at keeping their creative abilities in shape and maintaining their 'serious' reputation.

As to the local underground, it came to life after a long period of decline, but the position of these groups was sad. They were of no commercial interest to the collective farms, and no one else had time for them either. With literally no place to play, these groups decided on a desperate step—in the summer of 1983 they staged a spontaneous festival in the village of Yetsava (about 100 kilometres from Riga) without any pretence of official backing.

This event unexpectedly had significant repercussions in Latvia, compounded by the fact that one of the audience drowned near the festival site. Only in this way could the unacknowledged musicians attract attention. Officials recognised they had a problem at hand, and decided to solve it—such was the genesis of the country's second rock club, formed under the auspices of the executive committee of the Riga komsomol.

The club's membership was a mixed bag—Pete Anderson's nostalgic

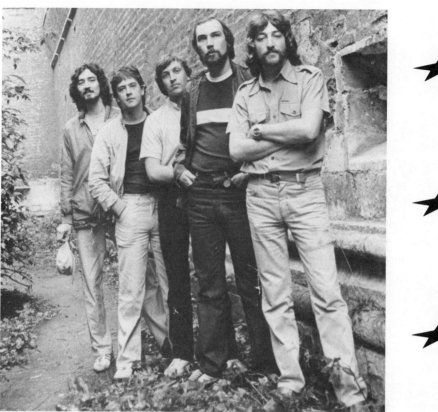

Poised to take the West by storm: Autograph with Alexander Sitkovetsky (front).

The venerable Time Machine in the Soviet far east, Vladivostok, in 1984.

Yellow Postmen . . . leader Ingus B extends his right palm.

Aquarium: Alexander Titov (new bass player), Boris Grebenschikov and Andrey Romanov (left to right) striding down Rubenstein Street in front of the Leningrad Rock Club.

Kino, featuring singer Viktor Tsoy, in concert in a Rock Club festival, in 1985.

A familiar scene: Spitball from Auction backstage with an admirer.

Centre in concert: on the left is Vasily Shumov, next to Sasha Skliar, now leader ot Moscow punkabilly band Va-Bank.

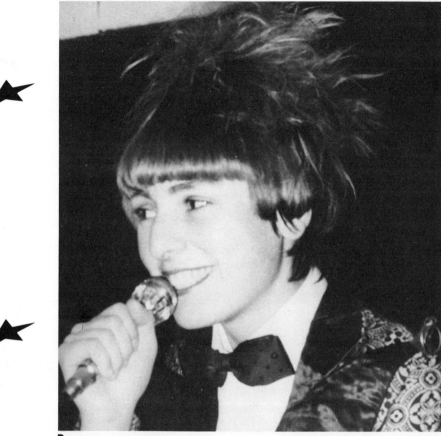

Bravo's Zhanna Aguzarova.

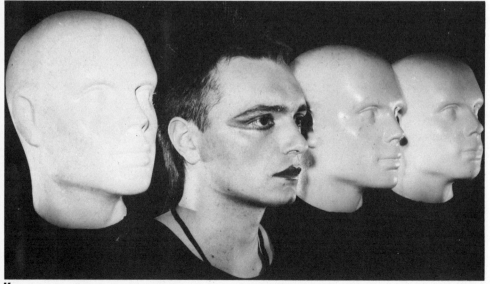

Kostya Kinchev of Alisa with some non-members of the band.

Joanna Stingray with the author in June 1986, immediately after the release of the 'Red Wave' album.

Aquarium in concert in 1986: (left to right) Boris Grebenschikov, Alex Lyapin and Seva Gakkel.

The unacceptable face of Soviet rock: Vova Siniy about to illuminate.

AVIA's most recent line-up with feminised brass.

Jungle, pictured in 1985, with Andrey Otriaskin at far left.

Front and back covers of the first Zoo cassette LP – a typical example of a Soviet underground tape.

The voice and hands of rock glasnost: Mikhail Borzykin of Televisor performing in Leningrad in 1987.

Antis on stage. In this scene actors dressed as druzhinniky (security police) attempt to carry an hysterical Algis Kauspedas from the staae.

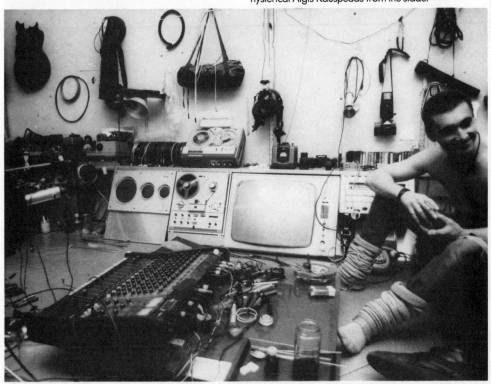

Alexey of Group B (Moscow's newest electronic group) in his home studio close to the Union Of Composers HQ.

Zvuki Mu pictured in Vilnius in October 1986. Leader Peter Mamonov, centre, draws on a cigarette.

The author at work in his room at his mother's Moscow apartment. (Picture: Peter Nasmyth)

rockabilly group Dope (renamed by request of the curators and subsequently known as Archive), a trio of Hindus with sitars and tabla, a satiric hard rock band called Too Late (with songs about the low salaries of engineers and the low quality of locally-made musical instruments), a free jazz ensemble called Atonal Syndrome, a psychedelic folk group called The Bridge, a noisy avant-garde crew called Zga and others. Two things united them—nonconformism and obscurity. It's worth noting that the Riga rock club had no space of its own. When the musicians called a general meeting, it was held in a courtyard near the Allegro Cafe . . . which was OK in the summer, but difficult in winter or when it rained. Even with its own club, non-commercial rock remained music for 'outsiders'. One curious consequence was that although Russians make up a significant portion of the population in the major cities of the Pribaltika, there hadn't been a single Russian-singing group either in the Latvian 'collective farm philharmonia' or among the participants in the Tartu festival. In the Riga rock club, though, Latvian and Russian bands came together because they shared the crucial common traits: a nonconformist style and lack of recognition.

Without question the best band of the Riga rock club was Yellow Postmen. Previously they'd been known as The Young Crimson Kings and, as the name makes clear, showed strong influences of King Crimson. However with the arrival of new wave their style changed radically; they dropped the heavy gear and became four prosaic looking lads playing on toy electronic instruments. The music was minimalist-monotone and simultaneously charmingly melodic. In fact, the music was similar to Riga itself—a large, grey city with a straight-laced German character but a kind of pallid delicacy as well. The Yellow Postmen sang about cafes that had closed, about suitcases, deep-sea divers and the fact that summer was ending. Their songs were built on computer-based rhythms and enjoyed great success in student discotheques until someone decided that their music was 'questionable', and the Postmen found doors closed to them.

The group Railroad offered some hope—17-year-olds, very loud, aggressive, dressed in metal regalia and dog collars. The singer, a natural Nordic blonde, shouted continuously at the audience to clear the centre aisle, as the railroad had to pass through there. They were original, but couldn't ever get it together to compose more than five songs. And so the punk idea didn't develop in Latvia. Railroad's drummer subsequently became one of Latvia's most interesting amateur film directors. His current project is a documentary on the up-and-down fate of three generations of Latvian rock, using as examples the careers of Pete Anderson, Martin Brauns and the Yellow Postmen.

Meanwhile, nothing at all was happening in Lithuania, the third and largest of the Pribaltic republics . . . nothing, that is, if we don't count having the best jazz and the prettiest girls in the country. Perhaps these circumstances hindered the development of rock music there.

7.

'Kids, oh kids!
We feel uneasy for you.
What is going on?
What are you doing?'
   —'The Photolab' by Centre.

IT HAPPENED GRADUALLY AND IMPERCEPTIBLY, but by 1983 the situation in rock differed dramatically from 1978. To start with, Western rock was much less popular and had lost its status as a cultural revelation or lifestyle model. The slang based on English words survived only among hardcore hippies and provincial punters, the stir over 'contraband' albums had quietened, home-made badges and 'educational' discotheques had disappeared. Moreover, Western rock had surrendered its position as a consumer item as well—the veteran favourites (Beatles, Queen, Pink Floyd, Rainbow) still enjoyed popularity, but new groups like Dire Straits, The Police and Duran Duran generated little interest. Russian rock groups singing in English were a thing of the past.

This vacuum in the musical consciousness of young people was filled by disco and syrupy Italian pop, on the one hand, and by rock made in the USSR on the other. The professional rock scene flourished. Time Machine's lustre faded somewhat—teenagers found them old-fashioned, while older fans rightly complained that their new songs were toothless and too slick. Autograph and Dialogue armed themselves with lasers, sequencers and other high-tech gear to fully satisfy lovers of art rock. The heavy metal side was kept up by Magnetic Band and a new group called Cruise, featuring the sensational guitarist Valery Gaina. From the same realm came a dreadful band called The Earth-men, who unified heavy metal heroics with the pomposity of official popular music and had the biggest hit of the period—a song called 'The Grass Of Home' about cosmonauts (unfortunately they lacked the kitsch to make it really funny). Carnival wandered prodigiously among Moscow's restaurants, but in the end they too made for the professional stage. Their music, however, maintained its variety show atmosphere and danceability in styles ranging from relaxed reggae to cocktail lounge ballads à la Bryan Ferry. Their singer, Alexander Barikin, was one of only a few Soviet rock stars with even a hint (a very modest hint) of sex appeal.

The restaurant scene also changed, and modern pop groups with synthesizers and light shows replaced the older generation of sleepy jazz bands. Many of the English-singing rock vocalists found a new niche in the restaurants.

The most promising group of the period was Speaker, created in early 1982 by Carnival's ex-guitarist Vladimir Kuzmin. They played dynamic, contemporary rock with artful electronic arrangements by keyboard player Yuri Chernavsky. They also possessed the best rhythm section in the country in the persons of drummer Yuri Kitaev and bassist Sergei Ryzhov (our answer to Sly & Robbie). Kuzmin was a multifaceted band leader. He played excellent guitar (somewhat similar to Mark Knopfler) and sometimes flute and violin; he sang in a high-pitched voice and worked hard at being a showman, changing clothes during concerts and acting out his lyrics. His stage manner and singing came off as a bit naive and not overwhelmingly competent, but this only supported his overall childlike image. He succeeded in his role as 'the boy next door' and was much more accessible than certain other heroes and 'geniuses'. The lyrics were neither controversial nor pretentious, but straightforward with a personal slant. A song in which the hero complains about his girlfriend rejecting him for a foreigner who gave her a pair of foreign-made jeans was especially successful. Even such harmless satire seemed fairly bold when played on the stage of a sports palace. In a certain sense Speaker filled the gap between the sterile philharmonia groups and 'street' rock. It was something fresh, and many saw Speaker as the successor to Time Machine at the head of the genre.

In 1983 the newspaper *Moscow Komsomol* conducted the first-ever poll of Soviet rock critics. (By this time almost all the youth newspapers had a pop music column. The small space allotted and the tiny remuneration were compensated for by the chance to give 'hot' information—concert reports, record reviews and so forth.) For the poll we approached approximately 30 journalists and other people active in rock from Moscow, Leningrad and Tallin. The Top 10 favourite groups were: 1. Speaker, 2. Time Machine, 3. Aquarium, 4. Autograph, 5. Dialogue, 6. Ruja, 7. Rock Hotel, 8. Magnetic Band, 9. Cruise, 10. Earthmen. My personal top three were Aquarium, Turist and Centre.

The third place finish by Aquarium, who up to this point had been denied the opportunity to tour and ignored by the media, would have been impossible to explain had it not been for a new phenomenon that appeared in the early eighties and is probably the most important development in the history of Soviet rock—home-made albums.

Sad as it may be, all that is left from our rock of the sixties and seventies are memories, photographs and a few odd newspaper clippings.

More weighty 'material evidence' does not exist. The music of Jesfers, St. Petersburg and many many others disappeared without a trace because nobody recorded it. (Thus it's difficult to confirm Gradsky's assertion that he was the first punk.) The random concert tapes of the time were of such quality as to make their preservation for posterity senseless. It's difficult to say why the recording issue, so obvious to everyone now, didn't concern anyone then. Probably there was so much going on day to day that no one bothered about capturing it for eternity.

The pioneer of home-made recordings was a Leningrader named Yuri Morozov. He never performed live. He worked nights as a sound studio engineer and put out an endless stream of albums (hard rock with insipid, 'cosmic' lyrics). He was active at this in the early seventies and recorded, according to rumour, almost 60 home-made albums.* But he never became a model for imitation and the few who knew Morozov's work considered him an eccentric loner.

The first genuine contemporary home-made album that became a prototype for others in format and design was 'Sweet N. & Others' by Mike Naumenko. Of course, naming one album as the first is debatable. In the late seventies the first decent sounding tapes of Time Machine ('Sun Island'), Leap Year Summer ('Prometheus') and Sunday appeared among collectors. But in my view these were compilations of relatively listenable concert tapes and random sessions, not fully-fledged albums. The fans were more involved in them than the musicians—it was the fans who named them. Makarevich feels that Time Machine's first worthwhile home-made cassette album came out in 1984. 'Sweet N. & Others' was, in actual fact, a regular store-bought reel of tape with room for 45 minutes of music and photographs glued lovingly and neatly on the cardboard cover (as a rule the musicians did this work themselves).

Everything was done with great seriousness, in proud observance of all the rituals and details of 'real' product (including writing 'Stereo' and the © and ℗ symbols). On the front cover was a drawing of an attractive nymphet in a cute hat (Sweet N. herself, we'll assume) carrying a record of Mike's under her arm while the latter gazes morosely after her. On the other side, naturally, was a list of the songs and the musicians and others who helped with the recording. Yes, this was the real thing, an attractive and 'finished' product. And it all cost only 10 roubles (which was approximately the cost of the reel, plus photo expenses, plus a bit for manual work with glue and scissors). It was called an album 'with design', and there would be precious few of them in circulation, maybe 20 or 30 at most. Musicians gave them as gifts (or sold them, which didn't make much difference) to their close friends, who in turn would give them to various friends and acquaintances to be copied, and so forth in geometric progression from tape player to tape player. Thus grew the quantity of albums 'without design'.

'Sweet N. & Others' passed unnoticed . . . due to insufficient ad-

*The home-made albums were cassette and reel tapes, not pressed records.

90

vertising, apparently. In 1981 two Aquarium tapes were released—'Blue Album' and 'Triangle'. The first differed from their usual acoustic concert set only in sound quality, but the second possessed all the signs of a specially prepared studio session, i.e. a conceptual unity in the songs, guest session musicians (jazz virtuoso Sergei Kuryokhin played piano solo), a mass of sound effects (reverse tape, pre-recorded sounds of birds, gunshots, etc.). The man responsible for the recording was Andrei Tropillo, sound engineer at one of the Pioneer* centres and producer of all Aquarium's albums (as well as numerous other Leningrad rock tapes). Tropillo was a true believer—he never accepted money from musicians and endured all the hassles aimed from above at his little two-track studio. These days he has eight-track equipment, demands unconditional subordination from the groups he works with and suffers from mild delusions of grandeur—but there's a grain of truth in his assertion that he "changed the course of Soviet rock." *Youth organisation for children of primary school age.

Home-made albums opened a new world, both for musicians and their fans. Our rockers saw the advantages of working seriously at recording and found they were able to make their music sound the way (or almost the way) they wanted to hear it; no more resorting to complaints about poor quality concert equipment. Further, they now had the opportunity to spread their music everywhere without the headaches of touring. They felt they were a part of show business, and even though it was partly a game (like the © and ℗ symbols on their home-made albums), still it was such an enjoyable game! (And much more realistic than playing Monopoly.)

Of course the idea of making home-made albums didn't just fall from the sky. Although Aquarium's releases were the most popular and influential, we should note, in the interests of fairness, that analogous artifacts were appearing simultaneously and independently in Sverdlovsk ('Expedition' by Urfin Juice,* 'Shagreen Leather' and 'Who You Are' by Track) and in Riga (the Yellow Postmen's debut entitled 'Bolderay Railroad'). Both Sverdlovsk groups were based on remnants of the defunct Sonance. Alexander Pantikin became disenchanted with avant-garde music and moved Urfin Juice towards hard rock, while Track played original, monotone new wave somewhat reminiscent of Devo. Unfortunately, the group broke up in 1983 after recording three albums. *Name of the anti-hero of a popular children's book.

In 1982–83 the taping fever took hold in all rock centres except Estonia, the only place where the local Melodia branch worked at keeping up with the happenings in rock music. A taste for the new action appeared unexpectedly among the professionals—'unofficial' albums by Speaker, Dialogue, Earthmen and even a few VIA bands appeared on reels. These groups' songs were remote from any censorship problems, but they had lost hope in Melodia (with good reason) and preferred the more simple method of spreading their songs.

Advertising such product proved not only simple, but also exceptionally efficient—the whole abundance of home-made music was playing not only in private apartments but also in discotheques, of which there were tens of thousands across the country. And each discotheque was enduring the same problem—an intensive struggle against 'Western influences' mandated from above. Specifically, the struggle was reflected in the setting of certain quotas for the discotheques' repertoires, such as: to play no less than 50 percent of songs by Soviet songwriters, no less than 30 percent by songwriters from other socialist countries, no more than 20 percent by Western songwriters. The figures varied in different locations depending on the liberalism of the local organs of culture.

Comic relief: Once I came upon a discotheque's official repertoire list, where I read the following entries: Brandenburg Concerto—J. S. Bach—G.D.R., followed by Symphony No. 5—L. van Beethoven—F.R.G. When I enquired about Bach and Beethoven coming from different countries, I was calmly informed that Bach was born in Leipzig, while Beethoven was born in Bonn, and thus the entries were perfectly accurate . . .

So roll over, Beethoven.

As a result of the struggle, the once trendy discotheque phenomenon began losing popularity—the public didn't want (or was simply unable) to dance to poorly recorded Soviet popular music that lacked the necessary drive. Meanwhile the real hits were being parcelled out by frustrated disc jockeys only in the prescribed miserly portions.

The boom in home-made albums proved a life-saver for the drowning discotheques. Finally the audience had Soviet music that satisfied their demands, if not in the clarity of its sound then at least in its style and character.

Songs from the 'albums on reels' immediately took up the lion's share of the discotheque repertoire. In the winter of 1984, while writing an article (that was never published) on the tape fever, I conducted a poll of the leading Moscow and Leningrad disc jockeys that yielded the following Top 10 of Soviet dance hits:

1. 'Hello, Banana Boy' (Yuri Chernavsky)
2. 'Kara-Koom'* (Circle)
3. 'Sweet Life' (Primus)
4. 'I'm A Robot' (Yuri Chernavsky)
5. 'Paper Snake' (Alla Pugachova)
6. 'The Stupid Starling' (Time Machine)
7. 'Moscow Vagabond' (Alpha)
8. 'When We Were 17' (Speaker)
9. 'Square Man' (Dialogue)
10. 'Doll' (Alliance)

*Name of a desert in Central Asia.

Only one of these songs ('Paper Snake') was ever played on TV, and one other ('Stupid Starling') appeared on a compilation album. The list is interesting from another point of view as well—it contains none of the pioneers of home-made tape making. What happened was that the discotheques quickly turned from passive users of the product into active clients who placed orders based on their own needs. Since the music of Aquarium, Kino or Centre wasn't terribly suitable for dances, the disc jockeys found more 'flexible' groups to give them the product they required. A real cottage industry for recording and duplicating tapes developed, and it was subordinate more to commercial than to artistic forces.

The laws in force were strange: the musicians earned nothing but fame and glory, while all the money circulated among the producers and distributors. The latter had little difficulty maintaining a monopoly since the sound studios (i.e. any place a mobile, enterprising producer happened to set up his Revox or a simple quadrophonic deck remade into a four-track recorder) were few and concentrated almost entirely in Moscow. The master copy of each new tape was duplicated in hundreds of copies and sent straight away (for sizeable sums) to clients in the provinces, who in turn made up their expenses by making and selling more copies.

A large part of the discotheque rock was obvious junk; like dance hits all over the world, these songs stayed on top for a couple of months and then disappeared forever without a trace. Exceptions to this rule were the albums 'Rock'n'Roll Journey' by Primus and 'Banana Islands' by Yuri Chernavsky. Primus (ex-Integral guitarist and vocalist Yuri Loza plus rhythm box and sequencer) played electronic rockabilly with lyrics where the banality of the language and images made an odd combination with the 'forbidden' subject matter (drunkenness, dissolution, and even hints of homosexuality). I remember that when I first heard Primus I guessed they were some VIA group given official mandate to play punk rock (as they imagined it to be). In fact, Primus were a poor man's Zoo—superficial and simplistic, lacking the authenticity and irony characteristic of Mike. However, there proved to be an awful lot of 'poor men', and Loza's album was a big success, while the song 'Sweet Life' became nothing short of a legend:

'There's a girl in the bar today,
The girl is fifteen years old.
Next to her is an undernourished guy,
They're sharing a single drink.

Though they were told not to,
They've spent a week's allowance
For breakfast on a couple of cocktails
And a pack of cigarettes.

The girl of course is glad
That she's wearing such intense pants.
She's tickled by all the glances
(The ones aimed below her belt).

The girl gazes wearily,
As if she doesn't care.
You know, she's seen and tried
It all long ago.

And such is life!
So live and don't worry.
Too bad life isn't this way
Every single evening.

Mama, hold on! Papa, watch out.
If life gets this way every evening.'

'Banana Islands' was no less popular and much more engaging. It's one of the cheeriest albums in Soviet rock, recorded by one of the saddest looking performers. Yuri Chernavsky is skinny as a rail with awkward movements; he wears enormous black glasses, speaks with a thick 'industrial' voice and looks basically like some kind of mad professor from a video clip. He was not young (born in 1947) when 'Banana Islands' came out and had already played sax and keyboards in a dozen jazz bands, VIA and rock groups (the last of which was Speaker). He had also earned himself a reputation as one of the best arrangers and the leading expert on electronic music in the country. The majority of our well-educated keyboard players approached the synthesizer almost the same as a piano, playing with fantastic dexterity in standard registers. Chernavsky studied the tonal possibilities of the synthesizer and tried to create unheard-of sounds. Usually he mentions Peter Gabriel as the musician who influenced him most, but his work is closer in spirit to Thomas Dolby and Yello. It has lots of humour.

'Banana Islands' was Chernavsky's first solo project, recorded with help from Vladimir Matetsky (formerly of Good Buy) and the Ryzhov-Kitaev rhythm section. It was a collage of styles (from rock'n'roll to computerised robot music) permeated with a driving rhythm and it stood head and shoulders above any other Soviet album, official or home-made, in its recording quality. Hard to believe that it was managed on just two tracks. A meticulous perfectionist, Chernavsky in the end couldn't find a suitable vocalist ("They all sing falsely.") and was obliged to perform the songs in his own weird voice, which in its pure form sounds almost like a Vocoder.

He didn't extend notes; his singing was more like reciting, and he communicated the subtlest intonations magnificently. His whole manner was like some kind of peculiar Russian rap. The lyrics didn't stir up any arguments—both the high priests of 'underground' philosophy and the official pop song poets happily accepted them as an amusing curiosity, a combination of children's verses and absurd paradoxes, songs about a tiny boy living in a telephone wire saying 'tu-tu-tu' to all the people whose conversations he interrupts, or a robot who goes crazy after being plugged into the wrong socket and sadly asks to be switched off. Chernavsky's lyrics were really very clever, and in one song a sad and serious meaning broke through the customary camouflage of humorous nonsense:

> 'I open my door and
> Step out to the horizon,
> To disappear with the sunset
> And fall straight to hell.
> But before I can take one step,
> Thousands of people come running up
> With papers in their hands,
> Papers in their hands,
> Papers in their hands!
> When I'm alone,
> Don't look after me.
> I'll do it myself!'

Towards the end of 1983 the easy-going era of rock music's happy commercial exploitation suddenly came to an end—it turned out that leaving the rock musicians in peace to look after themselves was not in the plan. It started with a campaign in the press; newspapers came down hard on rock groups for their 'greyness', 'bad taste' and 'lack of ideals'. As examples of mediocrity they cited the VIA (who had nauseated just about everyone by that time, making the criticism convincing). But a resolution adopted by the Ministry Of Culture shortly after the spate of articles appeared, was directed not at the truly 'grey' non-talents of VIA, but at the rock groups. The key point stipulated that henceforth 80 percent of the repertoire of any professional group should consist of songs written by members of the Union Of Composers.

Thus it became clear who was really behind the campaign: the Union Of Composers, an elite and very influential organisation whose ranks united both the academic composers and the official popular music songwriters. Members of the Union (there are only 3,000 across the country, including a large number of critics and historians of classical music) enjoy significant privileges in terms of releasing records, winning commissions to write film scores, getting advertisements in the media and so forth. The state buys from them an endless flow of operas, ballets and songs, many of which (fortunately) no one ever hears. In other words, they are supported in such a way that they earn as much money as possible.

But they were indignant nonetheless! Until the seventies, their monopoly was absolute. Then there appeared from somewhere these questionable young people with electric instruments who dared to claim that they too, could write songs. The Union Of Composers stood up for its privileges—no room here for outsiders. In 1973 David Tukhmanov joined the songwriters' section of the Union's Moscow branch . . . after which not a single new member was admitted for over 10 years. Small surprise then, that the members' average age is around 60. From time to time these angry composers have sallied forth from their ivory bunkers to shame rock, beat, pop art (they thought it was a type of music) and scruffy youth in general through the press and TV. The main accusation—rock musicians are 'illiterate' charlatans; people without special education cannot (or, as was sometimes asserted, don't even have the right to) compose songs. The crowning argument in their arsenal, which was supposed to produce the stunned silence of submission, was that 'some of them can't even read notes!' And yet despite this incompetence, music by the young songwriters gained more and more popularity (while the public increasingly regarded the songs of Composers' Union members as anachronisms).

With the appearance of philharmonia rock at the beginning of the eighties, this position became blatantly obvious. For all their esteemed titles and privileges and the unshakeable loyalty of TV and radio, the 'educated' composers were losing popularity, prestige and income. (Authors' royalties are paid for TV and radio broadcasts, for public concerts and for performance of songs in restaurants and cafés. The Union members maintained their lucrative monopoly only on TV and radio.) They tried to compete with the young songwriters, but without great success—even slick arrangements couldn't make their antiquated songs sound contemporary. The rockers, despite their handicap, won the battle for the public's loyalty. And the Union Of Composers, unable to win a fair fight, took advantage of its extensive contacts to force pop groups into performing its members' outmoded compositions.

A less influential but equally vociferous faction of the anti-rock lobby were the so-called *pochvenniki*,* russophile-inclined cultural figures, mainly writers, who idealise all things associated with the patriarchal, rural history of Russian life. In particular, they are categorically allergic to anything 'unrussian' or urban, and in their publications they had a happy time bashing rock music, discotheques and t-shirts with foreign words printed on them. All of which, according to the *pochvenniki*, tore our youth from its 'Russian roots', caused it to forget its 'national pride' and 'great heritage', and plunged it into an abyss of shameless depravity. (Seems I heard a similar opinion on music from the well known rock critic Ronnie Reagan.)

*From the word for soil, *pochva*.

96

Winter, 1984. The professional groups are in a panic. Each must appear before a commission from the Ministry Of Culture and perform a new programme in which 80 percent of the songs are not their own. Carnival failed the audition twice and broke up. Time Machine scraped together a few numbers and nervously awaited their fate, sitting in Moscow without the right to tour. Autograph rehearsed a programme of instrumental quasi-chamber music . . . "We hope they'll make an exception for us." Vladimir Kuzmin found a cynical but clever solution—he declared himself a solo artist, and Speaker became his nameless back-up group. In this way everything remained as it was, and the Ministry Of Culture's draconian resolution didn't apply to him as a 'soloist'.

It was ridiculous. And bitter. You'd think that the establishment would be sounding a fanfare to celebrate the fact that teenagers finally had their own countrymen for idols, that for the first time in 15 years Soviet pop music and songs in Russian had won popularity and prestige among the youth. But the bureaucrats had their own perverse logic and their own conception of the people's interests. I remember one incomparable commission session. Cruise were to perform, and the group were well prepared. Various well-known musicians, journalists, directors and even several liberal members of the Union Of Composers had been invited, and for two hours they all sang praises to the talent, hard work, virtuosity and topicality of this fine band, Cruise. At which point the chairman of the commission, a deputy Minister Of Culture for the Russian Federation and former accordion player with the mannerisms of a neurasthenic, stood up and said approximately the following: "We're very grateful that such authoritative and esteemed specialists have given their attention to the work of this ensemble, and we hope that your warm words will help these young musicians in the future. For now, we feel that this group has not matured sufficiently for independent concert work." And that was that. "Why did he make fools of us like that if everything was decided in advance?" protested the composer David Tukhmanov, giving the wheel of his black Volga a melancholy turn on the way back from the session.

Tension grew not only in the philharmonias. The word 'rock' began to disappear from articles and it became necessary to resort to literary tightrope walking in the search for appropriate replacement terms—'contemporary youth music', 'electric guitar songs', 'popular dance music' . . . Publication of the critics' poll was delayed for three months. Finally it was printed, but with certain polishing: the number two group, Time Machine, and the number one vocalist, Alexander Gradsky, disappeared from the list without a trace. The newspaper editor's motive for exclusion was that "They arouse doubts among some of the leadership." It was very amusing that Aquarium remained on the list—'some of the leadership' simply didn't know who they were.

But soon this loophole closed too. In the spring of 1984 the second wave of the attack on rock commenced, and the main targets this time were not the demoralised professional groups, but the 'independents'. At long last the bands from the 'underground' had attracted serious attention! But not exactly the way they wanted.

As long as the amateur groups operated on a local level, they encountered only local problems. The boom in home-made albums made them not only famous, but vulnerable. The state cultural apparatus was thrown into confusion, having detected an alternative 'record industry' right under their nose. The immediate urge was 'Ban it!' and all means towards that end would have been adopted, except that the project proved unrealistic. It was impossible to forbid sound recordings and impossible to stop the copying and duplicating of the home-made albums, especially since they were listened to in the privacy of the home and at parties. Discotheques were the only defenceless link in the chain, and it was these long-suffering enterprises who bore the brunt of the present offensive.

Home-made rock tapes were christened with the provocative and sinister name *magizdat* (an analogy with the dissident literature called *samizdat**). It's unclear where the mysterious new 'black lists' suddenly appeared from and how they circulated with such lightning speed—no one knew their origins, nor how 'official' the lists were, but they enjoyed success with the type of petty officials who always feel more secure with some piece of paper in their hand to guide them. When indignant musicians and disc jockeys came to the cultural organisations for an explanation of the lists, it was explained that these papers had no official status and represented only the 'personal opinion' of certain people in the Ministry Of Culture. But this was made known only in Moscow, and since no official renunciation of the 'black lists' was ever made, some provincial culture officials are guided by them to this day! Practically all the well-known amateur rock groups were on the lists, under the heading 'ideologically harmful'. Today it all seems like a bad joke—many of the 'enemies' have become respectable professionals who release records and appear regularly on TV. But at that time it was sad and unfair. The 'ideological' harm was being done not by those who were banned, but by those who did the banning. Young people were denied their right of choice, musicians were denied their prospects for 'legal' development, and music was denied its future.

In March 1984 the newspaper *Komsomolskaya Pravda* printed an article of mine in which I wrote that it was stupid to outlaw rock groups, that they would only go deeper underground, that what was needed was to work with the musicians and 'cultivate' them. It was a very reasonable, harmless and liberal piece, written from an official point of view, in which the Leningrad and Riga rock clubs were cited as positive examples. But even this brought forth a frenzied reaction from the culture bureaucracy—after all, the article had implied idleness and incompetence on their part in acting on the principle that it's easier to ban

* 'Izdat' comes from the word for print or publish; 'sam' means 'by yourself', 'mag' comes from the word for tape recorder (magnitofon).

something than to do something positive. Soon I discovered that I, too, had been 'banned'. In every editorial office I visited I found sour expressions on colleagues' faces and heard the shattering words: "You know, the boss said that working with you is not recommended. There was some kind of memorandum. They even mentioned your regular pseudonyms . . . so it's serious."

The situation reminded me of Kafka's Joseph K. I couldn't find out anything, neither who had 'banned' me nor in what way I had been 'banned'. (I don't know to this day.) I could only guess. Colleagues and acquaintances brought me news of interesting, even flattering rumours about memoranda where I was called leader of the punks, an accomplice in some underground movement, an agitator of Soviet youth or just an unfit journalist who aped Western styles. I would have been glad to hear all this with my own ears from the original sources and pose a few questions, but no one summoned me anywhere. Such are the shortcomings of working freelance—you've got no steady boss to see to it that you're not neglected.

It was a time of senseless decisions, but the destructive effect was not great, since the demands of the culture bureaucrats proved so absurd as to preclude the possibility of effectively ensuring their fulfilment. Thus the professional rock groups got around 'the 80 percent resolution' one way or another. The discotheques continued to spin 'non-recommended' tapes (although inspectors visited now and then, resulting in scandals). I continued to have my articles printed in Moscow, under the names of my girlfriends, while in the Pribaltika (where the winds from the capital don't always reach) I continued to appear on television as if nothing had happened. Grebenschikov, Mike and other 'banned' Leningraders earnestly recorded new tapes in Andrei Tropillo's studio. On the whole it was an active and fruitful period, which confirms the well-known theory that the best rock is often made 'under pressure'.

The Moscow scene before 1983 was empty and boring. What few groups existed were mediocre. Sergei Ryzhenko, violinist and singer from Last Chance, remained the great unfulfilled hope. He began writing superb songs that his bandmates considered too 'coarse', and so he put together his own electric band, called Football. Ryzhenko is a powerful, theatrical vocalist and a master of 'situation' songs. He composed a new, rather sexy version of *Little Red Riding Hood*, a touching song about a small girl sent to an enormous grocery store to buy vodka, and others. Being a good stylist, he rarely portrayed his feelings and experiences in his own name (as our other new wave songwriters do), preferring to write from behind various masks:

'*Up in the morning at 6:30, as usual,*
The over-filled tram, a dirty word,
Milling around the gate.

The day passes like a fairy tale,
Then you hurry to the bar,
Everything's the same.'

Here he sings for the working class, although he himself never lived that life. This particular effort didn't inspire much confidence, because our intellectual rockers, even the drunkards and street fighters among them, have a totally superficial understanding of the working class. The main strengths of Ryzhenko's songs were their vitality and populist nature. It wasn't folk rock, but electric folk songs. Much later I heard The Pogues, and they reminded me of Football. Unfortunately, the group played only two or three concerts during their year together. After the break up Ryzhenko moved on to play violin with Time Machine, but they didn't want to play his songs either, and so he left the group two years later.

The first Moscow rock group of the new generation was Centre. The first I heard of them was their tape recorded in the spring of 1982. It was real garage rock—a swinging, cheap sounding electric organ plus sloppy guitar and untrained back street vocals. The song titles were 'Melodies Float In The Clouds', 'Stars Are Always Pretty, Especially At Night', 'Love Tango' and 'Strange Ladies'. Three aspects of Centre were interesting: first, the cheerful style; second, the abundance of excellent, really classic rock riffs (of which the early Stones, Kinks, Doors and Stooges would have been proud); and third, the remarkable vocabulary and richness of images in the lyrics, which were distinct from both the street-scene alcoholic attributes of the Leningraders and the ennobled symbolism of the Makarevich school (with its 'candles' and 'castles' and the like). Centre's lyrics were something different, a mixture of naive, fairy-tale romanticism (about Tahiti, princesses, witches) and down-to-earth, day-to-day prose (about airbuses, radioactivity, tennis shoes). For instance, a trip with your sweetheart to outer space ends like this:

'The seconds will become a century
Inside the palace made of meteor dust,
And when you return to earth
You'll write a feature about it—
If there are still newspapers
And the people haven't died in a war . . .'

You may rest assured that no other rock band ever used the word 'feature' in their lyrics.

But for their occasional dreaminess, Centre's songs were not dumb or escapist:

> '*Someone looks in the window*
> *At the bluish glow of the TV.*
> *Everything was decided in advance,*
> *For no special reasons.*
> *Dozing off in the night,*
> *Jumping from bed in the morning,*
> *The constant rhythm of the seven-day week.*'

They also had one of the most sentimental rock anthems ever:

> '*When the sharks of sex first*
> *Inhabited the oceans of love,*
> *The tender fins of mermaids*
> *Began to look like pistols.*
> *When the golden rockers*
> *Smashed their guitars and amps,*
> *It became clear—their*
> *Tambourines were beating a warning.*
> *SOS, everyone hears. SOS, you and I.*
> *A fairy-tale floats on the wind,*
> *A new land has been discovered.*'

Thus began the changing of the guard in Moscow's rock music. Up to now there had been nothing to fill the gap between the generation of Makarevich (born in the early fifties) and the new generation (born in the early sixties).

Before long I saw Centre live, in a dark and cosy basement that housed Moscow's best amateur theatre (the Southwest Studio). The band were all about 20 years old, dressed in neat suits; their leader, the bass player and song writer, was named Vasily Shumov—the ideal name for a rocker.* On stage they were cool and unruffled, friendly but mysterious.

*The word for noise is *shum*.

That summer I took them to the unforgettable Vyborg festival, and the first appearance of Moscow's new wave was a triumph. Centre played with power and concentration and gave the weakened Leningrad bands no chance. A few months later, in November 1983, I decided to organise a major showcase for them in a respectable 1,200-seat hall using Dynacord equipment that we rented with great difficulty, and attended by a slew of important guests, including the press, TV, composers and rock stars. I wanted to prove to them all that there was life after Time Machine, that there was a real new wave of talented young musicians.

I arrived at the Palace Of Culture 40 minutes before show time and came upon a distressing scene in the band's dressing room: a table full of empty vodka bottles and four comatose creatures. Only the fifth, the young rhythm guitarist Andrey (son of the famous avant-garde composer

Alfred Schnitke) showed any signs of life—he proposed that we finish off the remaining bottle.

What had happened was that it was the drummer's birthday. The choice now was to either cancel the show or hope for a miracle. With difficulty I revived my musicians and asked them to get ready to take the stage. The concert that followed was unprecedented—they sang wide of the microphones and their hands missed the keyboard and guitar strings. Fortunately no one fell down. It was a catastrophe, of course. Few understood that they were completely drunk, though all agreed that they were very bad. The incident shows why Centre, despite their rare virtues, were never especially popular: they were always genuinely indifferent to success.

Centre's unpredictability was manifest not only in their behaviour, but in their music. Vasily Shumov was obsessed with the most unexpected ideas and influences, including Soviet popular music kitsch of the thirties and sixties, the prose of Edgar Allen Poe and the poetry of Arthur Rimbaud, turn-of-the-century Russian decadence and Joy Division. Remarkable that given all this, Centre didn't acquire a reputation as eclectics.

In 1984 the group entered a 'conceptualist' phase. They recorded two weird home-made mini-albums that contained a couple of 'regular' songs but featured super-short musical sketches. For example, 'Education':

> 'Mama said: All your girlfriends
> Have settled down now.
> Mama said: You're not getting
> Any younger, you know.
> Mama said: I don't want to see
> That bum in this house again.
> Papa said: You'd better watch out!
> Papa said: Leave me alone . . .'

Or 'Flash' (with a clavichord accompaniment in Renaissance style):

Male voice:	'Ivanova!?'
Female voice:	'Here, sir!'
Male voice:	'Flash on the right!'
	'Yes, sir!'
	'Flash on the left!'
	'Yes, sir!'
	'Flash on the right!'
	'Yes, sir!'
	'Flaaaaash!!!'

(Commotion, the sound of a misfire, the frightened voice of the girl: 'Oh, no!', the melody plays on.)

Difficult to say what all that means, but it sounds like a civil defence training lesson.

Centre didn't find any immediate followers. The capital's amateur scene was full of variety, but boring. The fans also seemed a bit lost. The prestige of the professional rock groups fell in comparison with the recent rage. There were no striking new trends, either in music or in fashion. The most lively mass phenomenon among Moscow teenagers was rooting for the local football teams. Crowds of kids roamed the city in identical red and white (Spartak) or blue and white (Dynamo) scarves, leaving corresponding graffiti in their wake on walls and pavements. The football seemed quite mediocre, but rock was no more inspiring.

A sensation finally happened at one concert in December 1983 in a large café/discotheque adjacent to the Olympic cycle racing track. Various groups performed. Centre played a lacklustre set and left the stage without acknowledging the applause. The audience was waiting impatiently for the DJ to spin the 'Flashdance' theme or something from 'Thriller'. Instead, four fellows dressed in fifties stilyagi-style stepped on stage and played a strong cover of Madness' 'One Step Beyond'. During the sax solo I established that the band were called Bravo. I recognised Yevgeni Khavtan on guitar immediately, as he had played previously in the band Rare Bird. Fragile and frightened looking with curly hair and a baggy suit, he looked a lot like the young Charlie Chaplin. When the instrumental intro set was over, a young girl in a suede mini-skirt and leather jacket (that was obviously cut for someone else's shoulders) flew onto the stage. For a second I pitied her—Barbra Streisand with her big nose would have come off looking like a Barbie doll next to this bird. But a second later the ugly duckling turned into an absolutely exquisite creature. She sang and danced as if she'd been locked away for a year; her eyes were on fire. The audience flipped, and this was something worth flipping over.

Of course, we'd had lively stage shows before Bravo (especially when the musicians had had a lot to drink), but this . . . a girl seemed like a revelation. Soviet rock is blatantly 'de-feminised'. With the exception of a pair of purely decorative VIAs, there have never been any women's bands, and the individual women musicians could be counted on your fingers. I remember the bass player from Integral and two Estonians, the pianist Anne Tüür from In Spe and the vibes player Terye Terasmaa of $E=MC^2$. As for singers, there were Aiva Braun (Sipoli), Nastya Poleva (Track) and Larisa Domuscha (Johnathan Livingston, a minor league Leningrad band), but none of them played a leading role in their bands. One could spend a long time figuring out why things were this way; I think old Russian traditions were to blame. In any case, Bravo broke with those traditions. Their girl stood out front and centre and dominated everything around her. Her remarkable stage personality, a mixture of prima donna and hooligan, transformed her unassuming twist into something deeper and more arresting.

The singer was Zhanna Aguzarova, an ambitious provincial girl who had come to take Moscow by storm but failed her entrance exams to the theatrical institute. She had nowhere to live and nothing to do, but didn't want to leave the capital. Someone gave her Khavtan's number, she called him from a phone booth and said that she wanted to sing. "She came over, sang some kind of improvised blues number, and we were all stunned." On the spot she dreamed up a prestigious sounding life story—that her name was Ivana Anders, that her parents were diplomats living abroad. It was very childish, but only gave witness to her fine acting abilities—no one among her musicians or even close friends ever doubted for a minute that she was anyone or anything other than what she said she was.

Bravo conquered Moscow in one night. Proposals from 'amateur' managers poured in from all sides, and the group set off to blaze a trail through the capital's cafes, clubs and student dormitories. Alas, the difficult times of 1984 were just around the corner, and Bravo's tour didn't last long. One of their concerts was interrupted by the militia, who raised questions about the legality of the five-rouble admission tickets being sold at the door. The group's equipment was confiscated and further concerts were declared 'undesirable'. (Fortunately the group had managed to record a good home-made mini-album before this setback.)

In March, many of the leading acts in the Moscow amateur scene (Chernavsky, Alliance, Alpha and others) were filmed by Leningrad television in the city's main discotheque, a place called Neva Stars. This was Bravo's television debut. Zhanna sang 'White Day'. She was wearing soiled white ballet slippers, and the uninitiated audience listened as if in a trance:

> 'I believe the night will pass, the gloom will disappear,
> I believe a day will come, all in sunlight.
> I will join in the joyous day, a prodigal son,
> And say, "Here I am, hello world." '

On the way home, as we were already approaching the railway station, Zhanna suddenly latched onto my elbow and said plaintively: "Let's stay in Leningrad. I don't want to go back to Moscow . . ." Of course we left all the same, and a few days later she was taken into custody by the militia. It turned out that crazy Zhanna, for fear of seeing her legend debunked, had made false identification documents for herself under the name Ivana Anders, and the forgery had been exposed. Bravo's equipment was returned, but the singer was detained. They sent her to Siberia . . . no, not in that sense. Siberia was just where her parents were living and working at a forestry processing plant (and suspecting nothing of their daughter's escapades). The big hope of Moscow rock was silent for a year and a half. In Siberia Zhanna entered a regional competition for young performers and won first prize, which was reported in the local press.

Meanwhile in Moscow a new rock attraction, a band called Zvuki Mu,* had made itself known. Peter Mamonov (born 1951), balding with gaps between his teeth and a tremendous scar next to his heart from an enormous file saw, began writing songs in 1982. I'd known him for 10 years before that as a witty drunkard, wild dancer and failed poet. Once he came to my flat with a guitar and sang for me. It was extraordinary, amazingly funny and potent; maniacal two-chord polka rock performed in screams, hisses and howls. The lyrics dealt mainly with Peter's personal experiences, evoking the painful relations between him and his sweetheart.

Before long he put together a group with his equally good-for-nothing younger brother Alexey on drums and a tall, phlegmatic keyboard player named Pavel. I was going to solo on electric guitar, but the affair got too serious—constant rehearsing—and I withdrew. Zvuki Mu's saving benefactor proved to be Alexander Lipnitsky, a common childhood friend of ours, a good-hearted and enthusiastic 'old hippie' who sacrificed his collection of antique art to buy instruments and equipment for the band. He began learning to play bass from scratch.

Zvuki Mu's first performance (February 1984) took place at the school where Mamonov and Lipnitsky had studied 20 years before. Both had been expelled then for bad behaviour, and the second time around the grown-up hooligans behaved no better. Peter proved to be a raving, epileptic showman who made David Byrne look rather boring by comparison. (Not my opinion, but that of some American acquaintances.) The level of grotesqueness and abnormal energy in his visual presence compared with the best work of Peter Volkonsky, but Mamonov's manner had a distinctly Russian flavour. He portrayed himself, but in a hyperbolic form—a mixture of street jester, gallant riff-raff and forgetful, bitter drunk. He would strike a showy pose and suddenly fall down, or foam at the mouth like a lunatic, or make unambiguous sexual motions before suddenly transforming into a pensive, serious figure. A brilliant, faultless actor! The public unanimously proclaimed him a schizophrenic, innocent on grounds of insanity. But in fact it was all calculation on Peter's part.

The songs sounded interesting now with electric arrangements—rock minimalism wedged into traditional, everyday melodies from blues and the waltz. Peter defined his own lyrics as 'Russian folk hallucinations', a stream of incoherent psychedelic images and obsessed delirium

at the edge of consciousness (the distinguishing feature of Soviet psychedelia being that it's based not on drugs, but alcohol):

> 'I'm getting sleepy, I lie down in bed,
> The bed squeaks and shakes under me,
> And at night my only wish is that
> No one will wake me come morning.'

Another song:

*Mainstream
singer of patriotic
songs who looks
like a statue and
is constantly on
television.

> 'I've completely lost my mind
> And all because of red wine.
> At night I don't sleep at all,
> At night I like to get tight.
> At night Kobson* sings to me.
> I can't tell, where am I and where is he.
> At night all colours are terrifying,
> All equally black.'

And so forth. There's no special meaning or originality in the lyrics,
but taken all together it works. The audience laughed hysterically, but
probably more in horror than amusement. Previously they hadn't been
put through the likes of this by a singer.

In July Zvuki Mu tried giving a concert on Lipnitsky's birthday in
a small open square in a little town of dacha cottages, but before the
start some militia cars drove up and it was necessary to transfer the
festivities to 'private territory' (the birthday boy's dacha). Later I heard
that in the Ministry Of Culture Zvuki Mu's attempted public concert
had been appraised as a serious subversive cultural diversion and there
was much congratulation for having prevented it from happening.

The rock backlash of 1984 continued unabated, and concerts without
official authorisation were halted for almost a year. A summer tour by
the Italian group Matia Bazar, the first Western new wave group invited
to the USSR by Gosconcert, was small consolation. The show had
computerised music, post-modernist stage design, decadent costumery
and vocals à la Siouxsie.

Locally, the only oasis where rock continued to blossom was Leningrad. In May 1984 the rock club conducted its second festival, and
the new bands left the veterans behind. Viktor Tsoy presented the
electric Kino (without Rybin, who had disappeared). It was a tight post-
punk quartet. They performed, among other songs, 'Nuclear Free Zone',
one of the few genuinely popular and sincere anti-war rock songs.

> 'Strong as my flat walls may be,
> One person's shoulders can't hold them all up.
> I see a house, I pick up some chalk,

There's no lock, but I hold the key.
I declare my house a nuclear-free zone!'

Even this drew angry criticism from sources who branded it 'spineless pacificism'.

A new band called Televisor made a nice pairing with Kino. As usual with Leningrad rockers, the lyrics were more interesting than the music (mainstream new wave plus a bit of reggae that all sounded a bit raw and under-rehearsed). They began their set by smashing a big cardboard TV screen on stage, and it was no empty gesture. Televisor played with real fervour. Their leader, the singer and keyboard player Mikhail Borzykin, was clearly influenced by the poetry of Boris Grebenschikov, only he was younger, more emphatic and nastier. One excellent song about Leningrad's *fartsovschiki* caught my attention:

> 'He knows what's in fashion,
> He's studied the business.
> He needs no god,
> He believes in his wallet.
> Satisfied with himself,
> But unhappy with everything else.
> If only he had his way
> He'd fly away for good.
> Always a bit bitter,
> A clever, simple man.
> The favourite of false women
> Who are corrupt like him.'

An exact likeness, including his mention of the dream of our black marketeers and prostitutes—to leave for the West. Borzykin was full of sarcasm, but also hope:

> 'At the piano it's just me and the snow,
> The black and white keys wait for spring to come,
> Even if there's not enough paint in this dream,
> I still haven't forgotten colourful dreams.'

It was uplifting but at the same time painful to hear these songs and see the audience's enthusiasm while thinking about the overall situation in rock. How could this music be put on a list and written off as 'ideologically harmful'? And when would spring come?

The group that made the strongest impression on me at the festival was Jungle. We had never had real instrumental rock (all the fusion muzak so adored by our commercial jazz men and music school students doesn't qualify in my mind). Jungle filled this gap, and how! From the moment I heard Jungle that day at the festival, Andrey Otriaskin took over first place on my list of best Soviet rock guitarists. He played a home-made guitar with all the stops pulled out on the flange and produced the most improbable sounds, playing rhythm and lead and 'noise' parts simultaneously. Stylistically it was a kind of frantic free funk with unexpected atonal changes and explosive rhythm. I remember it got me so wound up that I shouted to my colleagues on the judging committee that it was the best music heard in Leningrad since Shostakovich.

Later backstage, Otriaskin told me that he worked as a janitor in the conservatory, which seemed perfect. Jungle showed the rock club what real uncompromising music was all about. Unfortunately Jungle remained alone—popular new English records (Police, Soft Cell, UB40) were exercising a stronger influence.

Incidentally, a new important factor from the realm of 'Western influence' was video. At first VCRs were a preserve of the elite, but gradually the horrendous prices fell (at one time a VCR cost between five and seven thousand roubles, almost the price of an automobile), more and more decks appeared, and eventually even poor musicians had access to them, either through more well-to-do friends or even by pooling money to buy a machine as part of a group. Video mania broke up the traditional forms of home merry-making (only temporarily, we'll hope). Instead of an evening based around the table, with frequent breaks for dancing, guests now deployed themselves around the monitor and silently watched. As a prestige item, video tapes pushed foreign records into the background, and as a result people began bringing them in less frequently from abroad (though prices on the market didn't change). It goes without saying that all these minor inconveniences were compensated for by the new input of information that video's presence offered. We were now able to see 'in motion' that which we'd previously only listened to or read about—Woodstock and Altamont, Bruce Springsteen and Talking Heads. Video gave our musicians' consciousness a real jolt and, naturally, inspired them to try new tricks.

The next phenomenon to appear in the Leningrad rock club was Kostya Kinchev, and he was the first Soviet rock star whose visual presence showed some video style. He lived in Moscow and wrote songs but found the right partners only in Leningrad, in a middling rock club band called Alisa.* With its new frontman Alisa attracted a lot of attention in the autumn and then, as was expected, caused a sensation at the third Leningrad rock festival in the spring of 1985. Kostya has fluid and expressive gestures, a large mouth and bulging eyes, and onstage he looked almost like Nina Hagen. He spooked and snake-charmed the audience, stretched his black-gloved hands to the crowd, moaned, whispered and parodied in rap style. But above all, he was sexy. The forbidden fruit celebrated in song by the awkward looking Mike was presented here in flesh and blood.

*Russian pronunciation of a western name 'Alice'. The one who inspired the band's name, of course, visited Wonderland.

Paradoxical as it may seem, Alisa's lyrics (written by Kinchev, as was the music) had nothing to do with sex. On the contrary, they were a mixture of social satire and committed messianic bravado. Kinchev's alter ego was the hero of his song 'Experimenter':

> 'The experimenter, in motion up and down
> He walks streets of his own design
> He just got up, he's neat and clean
> He's straight as a vector and
> Stands like a fortress.
> The experimenter, in motion up and down
> He looks in the direction of his chosen goal
> He knows the answer, he's fully composed
> He lays out the path for other generations.
> The experimenter, in motion up and down
> He sees the horizon where others see a wall
> He believes he's right, he's sure of his idea
> He hits the mark in every trial.'

Kostya Kinchev was not afraid to take upon himself the role of 'mouth-piece' for his generation or opener of new horizons. He did away with the use of hidden irony, the ambiguous, equivocal mode of expression so characteristic in our rock and armed himself instead with the most resounding words, the most passionate appeals—everything that our sceptical audience sarcastically calls 'enthusiasm'. The heroic tone of his lyrics might make one think of an affinity with official komsomol anthems, but the musical and visual context, of course, transport them to a different dimension. And this inspired people remarkably; it turned out that the rock crowd had tired of its own social superfluity and inferiority and needed slogans and leaders. Kinchev's songs were titled 'Energy', 'My Generation', 'A Wave Is Coming' and 'We're Together':

> 'The initial impulse, the ball is in play
> A search for contact, the searching of hands
> I've begun to sing in my own language
> I'm sure it was not something sudden
> And I write verses for those who
> Don't wait for answers to today's questions.
> I sing for those who follow their own way.
> I'm glad if someone has understood me—
> We're together. We're together!'

The verses sounded timely. The freeze spread to Leningrad. Aquarium, Kino and especially Zoo were often being criticised in the press. The third festival proceeded in a fairly nervous atmosphere—in the presence of observers from the Ministry Of Culture. Only selected members of the rock club were permitted to take photographs and make recordings of the concerts.

Aquarium played the festival with the well-known avant-garde saxophonist Vladimir Chekasin. They were received coolly and afterwards decided to be done with 'experiments' for good. Strange Games were brilliant (in what proved to be their final appearance), playing a clever interpretation of the popular wartime anti-fascist song 'Baron von der Pshik'.* They broke up soon after the festival. Jungle played a more introverted, semi-acoustic set but were good all the same.

*Means 'nothing' in slang.

An excellent performance was given by the big band Popular Mechanics. The orchestra's director and composer, free jazz pianist Sergei Kuryokhin, collected around 30 people on stage. Among them were all the members of Strange Games, Boris Grebenschikov, Viktor Tsoy and all standing members of Leningrad's bohemian artistic community. The entire crew was divided into sections—jazz (brass instruments), rock (electric guitars), folk (some kind of elongated Caucasus horns), classical (a string quartet) and 'industrial' (sheets of metal, saws, etc.). The half-hour composition they performed was entitled 'No Matter What You Feed The Captain, He Still Looks Towards The Forest' (Captain is Kuryokhin's nickname), and though it was noisy and seemed a bit formless, it was still entertaining. Unfortunately, Pop Mechanics didn't rehearse regularly and came together, in various line-ups, only a few times a year, right before concerts.

The best song at the festival, in my view, was by Televisor. It was called 'Your Television Is Talking With You':

> 'Two hundred and twenty cold volts.
> The system is reliable, won't break down
> And the evening will give you nothing—
> The programme is always the same.
> People are eating, they feel good.
> It's the age of electronic enjoyment.
> Someone here needs an electric shock—
> Then I'll feel an awakening.
> Leave me alone, I'm alive!
> I want to think with my own mind.
> I don't want to name heroes.
> I don't want to talk of blood.'

It was a contradictory time. The external pressure on rock generated a wave of protest. There were few concerts, but tapes were everywhere. Recordings from distant provinces enjoyed success—a hard rock band called Cloudland from Arkhangelsk and DDT, from Ufa, who sang bitter and angry songs about provincial melancholy and 'centralised'

110

hypocrisy. (DDT's excellent singer and leader, Yuri Shevchuk, soon moved to Leningrad due to friction with the local authorities.) Meanwhile, in Moscow, rock hadn't died . . . it had just gone underground. Groups were still recording their low quality home-made albums. This, for instance, from a bilious band called DK:

'You understand life is crap!
Laugh and be merry.
Everywhere you turn—wine.
Don't torture yourself—get pissed.'

In practical terms, such in fact was the main result of the 'banning policy'—there was no way out, and nowhere to go. But things couldn't remain that way; young people couldn't live on cynicism and bad faith, and the rockers' energy and talent demanded an outlet.

In September 1984 I arrived in northern Vologda province at the invitation of local television to do a talk show on rock music. It's an area of unforgettable beauty, with stately forests, still rivers and ancient monasteries. It's the 'heart' of the country. And there, in the town of Cherepovets, I met a 24-year-old named Alexander Bashlachev. He worked as a correspondent for the tiny local newspaper, listened to tapes by Aquarium and DDT and had once written lyrics for the one and only local band, called Rock September. He said that he had recently begun composing his own songs and offered to sing them. As I listened, my eyes widened—he was an amazing poet who concentrated all the love and pain of the universe inside himself. He was not really a rocker, more like an heir of Vladimir Vysotsky. But he had one song dedicated to Russian rock, called 'Time Of The Little Bells,' with the words:

'Every day times are changing
The cupolas have lost their gold, and
The bellringers have nothing to do
The bells have been cast down and broken.
So what now?
We walk around afraid of our shadow
In our own world
As if we're from the underworld.
If we're left without a big bell
That means it's the time of little bells.'

So, what now?

8.

'There's new press
In a rotten cover
New Music, new styles
A wave is coming—
So listen to the sound
Until the new calm is here
A wave is coming
A wave is coming.'
    —'A Wave Is Coming' by Alisa.

AS EVERYBODY PROBABLY KNOWS BY NOW, the long awaited new political strategy was proclaimed by Mikhail Gorbachev at the CPSU plenum in April 1985. Soon afterwards there emerged within the depressed and angry Moscow rock community a thrilling rumour that a rock club would be established within the capital. The whole idea seemed to be arranged by impeccably official organisations like komsomol, the City Cultural Department and the Trade Unions. None of the rockers felt any liking for these comrades, or even trust. Yet the thirst to perform and communicate was so strong that practically all the Moscow bands, including the dissenters from Zvuki Mu, applied for official auditions in the hope of joining the rock club. I had no involvement in these proceedings and, quite lightheartedly, left for Riga's seashore—as I usually do in April—to walk along the empty beaches before they become congested with the regular summer holiday crowds.

When I returned to Moscow I went to the House Of Peoples' Creativity, where the auditions were due to begin, in order to witness the event. At the entrance I was roughly stopped by a certain komsomol boss: "Where's your invitation card?" I shrugged my shoulders. "My name is Troitsky and everybody here knows me." The man called over two of his assistants and replied firmly: "Yes. We also know you . . . and very well. And it is just precisely because you are who you are, Troitsky, that you won't get into this hall." I didn't argue and went away. Thus, in this discouraging manner, did the new era open for me.

For the first time in many years I didn't go to Tartu in May that year. Turist had split up, Hardy Volmer concentrated on his main job—making cartoon films—and the organisers did not promise anything new or sensational. (The festival *Grand Prix* was won by Karavan, a commercial and lightweight reincarnation of Kontor. Peter Volkonsky presented a comic rock opera entitled 'The Green Egg' with an all-star cast and Paap Kylar played 'industrial' music in heavy metal thrash style

112

with some drummer colleagues. I saw it all on video after the event.) Instead of having a leisurely time in Estonia, Sasha Lipnitsky and I went on a small boat up the rivers of Northern Russia to explore old Russian roots. Rock has reached these places too: in the central park of the ancient town of Vologda we saw a local band called Calendar playing songs by Time Machine and Alpha to an enthusiastic dancing audience.

Straight from the North I went alone to Vilnius, the capital of the rock desert of Lithuania where I was invited to their first ever big rock festival, Lituanica 85. Vilnius is the nicest of the Baltic cities in my opinion, very beautiful, comfortable and somehow reminiscent of Prague, the sweet dream of my childhood, with its green hills, cathedrals and intimate cafés. It is a perfect place for painters and jazz men but a virgin land for rockers. The only flourishing branch of contemporary electric music there were the sublime synthesizer bands, of which Argo, led by renegade symphonic composer Giedrius Kuprevichus, was the most impressive. The festival didn't dent this lovely image; the best of the local bands was an instrumental keyboard quartet called—of course— Catharsis.

More intriguing were the delegates from other rock provinces. Post Scriptum from Tbilisi were upper class kids, including a nice female piano player, who played some funny and charming tunes à la early Beatles. Olis seemed to be the first Armenian rock group that has surfaced in 15 years: they sang in Russian, dressed like New Romantics and had obviously spent a long time listening to Men At Work. Did all this mean there was a new rock boom in the Caucasus? Unfortunately not. From conversations I had with musicians I learned that all was quiet on the southern front, and rockers still feel rather lonely there.

The new generation of Byelorussian rock was represented by a band called Metro who were technically neat but hopelessly average in style. And also the name . . . I've noticed before that banal names are irresistibly attractive to unimaginative rockers. The champion band names are The Mirror, Pilgrim(s) and Metro—it seems that every city has a band with these names. Also popular are Rondo, Nautilus, Stalker and Ornament. Manic striving after an international sounding name is probably best explained by a secret hope to become world famous.

Meanwhile, the Big Event was about to happen in Moscow—the Twelfth International Festival Of Youth & Students. Here I noticed the first signs of my rehabilitation: I was invited to the headquarters of the Festival's cultural programme to be told that my knowledge of rock was highly valued and I was asked to participate in the work of the Rock Music Workshop. It was easy to guess why the organisers felt uneasy about the Workshop: the Soviet side of it was mostly represented by ageing official composers and their ability to cope with Western punks or Rastas was doubtful indeed. Anyway, from the very first day of the

Workshop operation it became clear that the whole affair was completely formal and very boring, and the 'problem foreigners' had no intention of appearing there. So, with my conscience intact, I immediately escaped from the music centre to the streets of Moscow.

Here it was far more interesting. Despite the titanic attempts to organise and co-ordinate everything, it was absolute bedlam. There were dozens of concerts every day and almost no information on them had been circulated. Of course, there was no culture shock 1957-style but still we enjoyed many new and interesting experiences. Certain things that we knew before from papers, records and (sometimes) video-tapes appeared live before us. Many of the events were held behind closed doors (meaning that only accredited people or those with invitation cards could get in) and in semi-empty halls. But each of the main festival rock acts played one open air show before a genuinely public audience, mainly in the famous Gorky Park. To the surprise and satisfaction of the frightened komsomol people, the whole atmosphere of the festival was very quiet and peaceful. There was only one accident —when the crowd broke the barriers during a performance by an awful Yugoslavian HM band called White Button which caused their gig to be stopped. Besides that everything went on in a style of gentle curiosity, a certain formality and a lively exchange of souvenirs.

Misty In Roots were the first real reggae band ever to play in the Soviet Union. Natural Rastas with dreadlocks, they had a ritual ganja smoke in Red Square and were very proud of it. All of their concerts ended up in total mass dancing which is absolutely non-traditional for our frozen audiences. The second British band to come over, Everything But The Girl, were stylishly English, rather discreet and highly regarded by our musicians. But they weren't a smash. Ben Watt and Tracey Thorn were unlucky with their open air show in that it rained after a few songs, but they were shown twice on Central TV and immediately after the festival Melodia released their single (which still seems to be a bootleg since they received no money nor even a copy of the record!).

The hottest venues at the festival were the Cuban and Finnish national clubs. The Cubans arranged some all night dancing parties with some tremendous salsa bands—Afro-Cuba, Hiron and Irakere. As for the Finns, they not only got all the beer available in Moscow's hard currency shops* (alcohol was officially prohibited at the festival) but also brought the biggest and weirdest rock crowd of all, about 10 bands including hardcore punk, thrash and even an all girl feminist quartet. The greatest of them—still remembered with affection in Moscow even now—were Sielun Veljet (The Soul Brothers, though they now go under the name of L'Amourder), four absolutely wild guys with raised hair arranged with plastic flowers. Their music sounded a bit like Killing Joke and the show was a mixture of lunacy, sex and pure brutality. They rushed on stage like madmen, threw their instruments into the

*Shops selling western goods for western currencies, consequently inaccessible to the average Soviet citizen.

114

air (where careful roadies caught them), took their clothes off and dived into the audience, all performed to a hard and hammering beat. Some of their tricks were beyond my video experience and to see this live was just stunning. The most surrealistic experience of the whole festival was to watch Sielun Veljet's performance at the State Variety Theatre with its thick red velvet curtains and gold vignettes . . . it was as if The Butthole Surfers had invaded the Oval Room at The White House. But far more shocking and sad was the fact that these boys had so much more bloody energy and outrage than our musicians could ever dream of capturing. "We just can't breed bands like this," Kris Kelmi (ex-Autograph and now leader of Rock-Atelier) said with a sigh. "It's not even because it would be forbidden . . . we just cannot be like them." Well . . .

But there were other things that put us in a more optimistic mood. One example was the number one Polish band Lady Pank who have just signed a contract with MCA and released an LP worldwide. They appeared to be pretentious and were not very impressive at all, just like our own average rock band. Then there was Udo Lindenberg, the biggest international star of the Festival, who was OK and quite charming, but I wouldn't say he was head and shoulders above his look-alike Gunnar Graps. Soviet rock was represented by the calm and adult orientated professional groups (Autograph, Time Machine, The Stas Namin Group etc.) and even they survived the competition. So the first big confrontation between Soviet and world rock seemed to look pretty hopeful. "No . . . we are not so poor and underdeveloped as we used to think we were," said Stas Namin, and he was probably right.

Bob Dylan was the great white hope of the festival, but this was not fulfilled. He played a couple of songs in one big and very official concert and afterwards just vanished into the comfortable swamp of the Soviet cultural elite. It was said that he went to Georgia and Odessa. Some of his spiritual children—Makarevich and Grebenschikov in particular —desperately tried to find him, but with no result. Dylan once wrote a song that said we all have to serve somebody; in Moscow Dylan chose to serve somebody else.

The Festival ended with fireworks and a torchlight march, but life continued as ever. The spring of *perestroika** blossomed slowly but steadily. The most visible changes occurred in the fields of economy, public relations and the political and government line-up. The experiments and reforms in industry, trade and agriculture started to happen; the papers became far more interesting and informative. There was the new trend of *glasnost*, dozens of officials and ministers were replaced by younger ones. The whole style of relations between the people and the establishment was now more open and democratic.

The cultural powers were in a state of confusion and disorientation. They couldn't stage rock in the way they used to for four specific reasons:

*Gorbachev's new policy of 'reconstruction'.

1. In the political statements of the party much was said about the urgent need to approach the youth of the nation in realistic and informal ways, about studying its actual tastes and demands, about encouraging its spontaneous ideas—and here rock was one of the most important features.

2. Many subjects—like drug problems, alcoholism, corruption and the black market—that were once taboo now became widely discussed in the press and elsewhere. So now the rock bands (in theory) couldn't be condemned for touching on these subjects in their songs—on the contrary, they represented the fresh shifts of *glasnost*.

3. Not only social criticism but also such economic values as profit now became highly regarded, and the commercial potential of rock was obvious. Rock could help the cultural institutions to survive under the new profit-conscious economic policy.

4. The monumental anti-alcohol campaign meant not only prohibition and various restrictions, but also advocating some 'sober' alternatives for the drinking youngsters like clubs, discos, concerts and fan associations etc. Here again rock was an inevitable alternative.

Nevertheless, most of the old-fashioned cultural officials were still in their armchairs, and they were not eager to act constructively. The words 'initiative' and 'enterprise' still represented some doubtful and dangerous hazard to them, and all they would actually listen to were 'directions from the top'. So while there were no specific instructions from the Central Committee about rock music, the bureaucratic army just kept marking time in secret hopes that everything would remain the same and they could keep their cosy jobs. Because of that the Moscow rock club, or The Rock Laboratory as it was now officially christened, was still in limbo. None of the city's main organisations had the courage to take responsibility for 'underground' rock, so the laboratory still got no official status, no house, no leadership—just a list of about 40 bands ready to participate.

But anyway, the atmosphere was completely different compared to 1984: rock concerts had started all over the city, and there were also lots of strange and amusing events where rockers took part in general *tusovka* (see below) along with avant-garde poets, conceptualist painters, break dancers and weirdos of all kinds. The alternative arts people showed up with unprecedented solidarity and business-like energy. The 'wild style' artists painted backdrops for the new wave bands, avant-garde poets cried out their lines to the screams of saxophones and the kitchenware beat of free jazz, bizarre fashion designers showed their collections to the accompaniment of hardcore noise groups. With more freedom and space for exposure, the Moscow radical art crowd began to consolidate and work together.

It seems that each era is precisely described by the key slang words of that particular time. For instance, in the carefree, laid-back era of the early eighties the main word was *kaif,* which means pleasure, joy and getting high. 'The Kids Are Catching Their *Kaif'* was the title of a famous Aquarium song from 1981 (and also the title of my first article about this band). Later the most popular and characteristic word was *oblom* which meant a broken *kaif,* a rip-off or a failure. 'There's a tough *oblom* everywhere', sang Mike Naumenko in 'Blues de Moscou'. In the present day the queen of slang is *tusovka* meaning something's happening, some kind of mess, some activity. It may be idle or significant but it's always something interesting. The questions of the day are: 'What *tusovka* tonight?' 'Where do they have *tusovka?*' (which means . . . who plays the concert or opens the exhibition or celebrates a chic wedding?).

Rock *tusovka* peaked in January 1986 with the first Rock Lab Festival. In a modest hall of one of the pompous Houses Of Culture all the best Moscow bands got together and, surprisingly enough, there were quite a lot of them. Even the jealous observers from the Leningrad rock club were noticeably impressed—despite the awful PA.

Fortunately, all the old friends not only survived through the ice age but even stayed together. Zhanna Aguzarova had come back from the taiga* in the summer, attended musical college and continued singing with Bravo. Their image had not changed a bit, so the novelty value faded slightly but now they had a true legend behind them. Their new hit song started with the line: 'Put my heart into sulphuric acid'. Zhanna kept inspecting the wardrobes of all her friends in search of stage clothes, so I gave her my golden carnival tuxedo from schooldays and my old-fashioned skiing suit.

*Northern forests.

Centre played their last gig with their perfect garage guitarist Valery Sarkisian. Vasily Shumov fired him from the band right after the Festival with the words: "Unfortunately you're now playing too well for us . . ." Centre wrote a new song called 'The Signs Of Life' which I'd choose as an anthem for both the Festival and the whole situation. It started with a long and dreary introduction, then suddenly rushed into a short but very passionate finale:

> 'The nerves are somehow used to soporific pills
> But even in a cage
> A *panther is ready to jump out!*
> Venus is fading
> And the birds appear
> The birds—the signs of life
> The signs of life—Yeah Yeah!!!'

Zvuki Mu were by now head and shoulders above the rest. They played much better and their lyrics were less obsessed with alcohol. This was one of those rare occasions when they played their best and most suggestive song ever—'The Opener'—about a man who lived and died and left nothing behind except his name—Kolya—which he carved on a kitchen table with a can opener. The song the audience loved the most, however, was 'Grey Dove':

> *'I'm dirty, I'm exhausted.*
> *My neck's so thin.*
> *Your hand won't tremble.*
> *When you wring it off.*
> *I'm so bad and nasty.*
> *I'm worse than you are.*
> *I'm the most unwanted.*
> *I'm trash, I'm pure dirt.*
> *BUT I CAN FLY!'*

At this unforgettable moment Peter Mamonov used to make memorable and indescribable movements—like a cross between imitating a bird in flight and the convulsions of a hanged man squirming in the noose. The whole verse was yelled in ecstacy: all these anti-social junkies and geniuses of the underground with spiky hair and earrings saw themselves as 'grey doves'—loathsome and vulnerable but still more 'high' than the normal, well respected people.

Some new groups performed at the Festival, bands who had begun to build their reputations in the autumn of 1985. Brigada-S were second only to Bravo judging by their commercial abilities, a driving new wave boogie band with a very loose and aggressive front man called Igor Suhachov whose mean stage image was reinforced by a bandit-like demeanour. They were the last band to appear, winding up the Festival by engaging the whole hall in a sing-song:

> *'My little baby, stay with me.*
> *My little baby, I'm your playboy.'*

The word 'baby' was pronounced 'beibi' in the English manner. It was sort of silly but quite fun.

Then there was Nicolai Copernicus, a band that showed a very rare blend of good musicianship and fresh ideas. Long ago I noticed that if an amateur rock musician plays well he either joins a professional pop band or starts practising jazz rock. Copernicus, however, comprised well educated young performers (some students from the classical conservatoire) who nevertheless played modern radical funk against an eerie futuristic background wash (shades of Japan or The Cure).

Also worth a mention are Night Avenue, a duet comprising guitarist/vocalist Alexey Borisov and keyboard player Ivan Sokolovsky. They played to a pre-recorded background tape and sounded just like Soft Cell, although their conception was just like Kraftwerk. Both men are actually young scientists and on stage they resembled a pair of 'dehumanised' intellectuals. Here's an extract from a song called 'My Working Day':

> 'The institute is buzzing
> Like a beehive.
> The entrance gate's working strictly.
> Young employees go side by side.
> The offices are waiting for them.
> One can hear only the rustle of papers,
> And the voice from the radio intercom:
> "We work fast and co-ordinated"
> Says my colleague named Viktor.'

From any band, other than Night Avenue, such lyrics would sound like a joke, a mockery of typical 'socialist realism' style, but these men are so suggestive and serious that one can only ponder over how cunning they actually are. For certain songs they invited a guest vocalist, an ascetic looking thin blonde named Natasha, to join them and she was responsible for Night Avenue's best song:

> 'Oh, if I had died when I was a little baby,
> I wouldn't eat and drink and listen to music now.
> And my parents would have got a car long ago.
> They wouldn't have to give me roubles.
> They could have saved money.
> Oh, if I had died when I was a little baby,
> I'd have become a cupid and flown to Washington
> And told him not to start the war.'

The festival attracted favourable coverage in the press and the Cultural Department of Moscow City Council was—at last—approved as the official sponsor of the Rock Laboratory. Soon afterwards there were democratic elections for the Art Soviet of the Lab: all interested musicians participated and voted for Mamonov, Lipnitsky, Khavtan, Shumov and other nice people. Then the line-up of this board was approved by the officials . . . and it was a strange feeling because all these 'members of the Art Soviet' were completely illegal a year ago and had much trouble with the state.

I was also elected to the council and, for the first time in several years (in fact, since I went freelance in 1983) was given certain duties —attending auditions for new bands, signing (or not signing) their membership in the Rock Lab, and giving them advice. These frequent encounters with the problematic musical youth led me so far that in May 1986 I even appeared on stage as vocalist in an all-star band (with Aguzarova, Mamonov, Borisov and Shumov), performing the latter's rock-opera 'Rimbaud'. Fortunately the show's run was limited to one premiere performance.

It had been a long time since I had seen our professional bands, but suddenly there appeared an opportunity to see them all in one setting at a big and prestigious festival called Rock Panorama '86 which was organised by Moscow's City Komsomol Committee. It lasted for four days and, with the exception of Autograph and several Baltic bands, the whole Soviet philharmonic rock elite was there. What I saw at the Central Tourist Hall was both glamorous and sad: a parade of rich costumes, lighting effects, expensive western instruments yet a complete lack of raw energy or inspiration. Two kids who sat right behind me constantly discussed the labels on the sneakers that the musicians were wearing. That was a normal reaction, so bland and superficial were the bands.

The first thing that would offend an underground follower was the sheer banality of the lyrics. It was completely disheartening to listen to words from the stage that were so similar to the vomit-inducing VIA texts against which we raised the rock rebellion in the first place. When authors were credited I recognised the familiar names of infamous professional lyricists . . . so they've started to dig rock now! Relatively acceptable were Time Machine, Alexey Romanov (ex-Sunday) and Alexander Gradsky, but even their profound 'bard-rock' sounded boring and outdated, both in themes and words.

The music was even worse: the groups came and went but the sound was just the same. This was some kind of synthetic style practised by everybody—disco rhythm, smooth electro-rock arrangements and commonplace pop melodies. It seemed that the nightmarish Modern Talking served as a prototype for everybody. The bands believed so too.

The heavy metal groups were a little more convincing. Cruise kept playing endless hard rock guitar-dominated pieces in the manner of Ritchie Blackmore, this time around as a trio with a new drummer. There was also a sensational debut by Aria who showed off all the archetypal HM attributes: black leather, chains, metal crosses and heavy bracelets. From 50 metres they were indistinguishable from Iron Maiden! Such things never happened before with professional bands.

It was tricky for the HM bands to justify themselves since all wished to avoid accusations that they were 'propagating violence', thus their heavy riffs accompanied sweet pop lyrics (The Earthmen were especially good at this) which, of course, was quite ridiculous and even distasteful. Aria, on the contrary, didn't seek to hide their aggression or the gothic/fairy-tale symbolism but used them to good advantage. When they sang lyrics along the lines of 'Let's crush the thousand headed killer dragon . . .' they meant 'Let's struggle against war . . .' Their HM anthem 'Here We Forge The Metal' was nominally about the hard labour process in the smithy!

The only area in which the professional rockers had made significant strides was in stage presence: pyrotechnics, stage clothes, makeup etc. All this resembled the international video cliches so the Western correspondents were quite impressed. They judged Soviet pop by the dreary TV programmes and Melodia recordings and therefore considered the affair in a different light to myself. Nevertheless even the toy rockers from Panorama '86 had virtually no access to the mass media, despite these packed stadium concerts.

Bravo, the only amateur band in Rock Panorama '86 received the principal prizes of the festival but the rock establishment didn't acknowledge this punch on the nose. They were still self-satisfied and cared only about prestige, money and new equipment. Very few of them were interested in what was happening within the new generation of rock bands. "We sell out the sports palaces . . . what else do you want?" was their answer to my criticism. "Crisis? What crisis?"

I didn't feel a fiendish delight about Bravo's obvious victory over old bands. It was rather sad that the musicians of my age, my old comrades, seemed to sell out and calm down or 'put their teeth on the shelf' as we sometimes say. Just another inevitable generation gap, but a sad thing to witness, especially when it happens to people who shared the same idealistic hopes as the rock community.

We could finish the tale about the sixties and the seventies rock heroes in the style of a Charles Dickens epilogue . . . so, Alexander Gradsky remained an egocentric loner and author of pompous ballads and joined the Composers' Union. Andrey Makarevich, as a talented pop bard, kept singing edifying songs until old age, still entertaining his devoted followers and some nostalgic youngsters. Alexey 'White' Belov kept changing his restaurant bands but after so many years no one would go along to listen to him.

I'd be glad if the future refutes me.

I didn't bother to wait until the Rock Panorama laureates concert was over but left for another Tarfu festival. I anticipated no revelations there—just some pleasant relaxation and classy traditional music. These not so great expectations were fairly fulfilled. Rock Hotel added a brass section and played an immaculately stylish set in the irresistible Blues Brothers manner (with even the same instrumental introduction). Yuri Rosenfeld from Music-Seif confirmed his reputation as the country's most precise blues guitarist. Even Peter Volkonsky appeared less radical than usual; his surprise concept this year was a semi-parody interpretation of six Franz Schubert songs. The whole festival could have been compared to a comfortable limousine slowly cruising on soft springs along a smooth highway. As a temporary contrast to the permanently shaky state of Russian rock, this was quite nice.

Some new bands were playing on the fringe of the festival in the Agricultural Academy. Designer punks Big Sister (including some ex-members of Turist) loudly proclaimed themselves the founders of a new style called 'primi-futu' (primitive-futurist) but lacked any drive or playing abilities. These qualities were inherent in T-Klass (Propeller with a fat new vocalist) but they played simple heavy metal. The band I preferred was Modern Fox, a small big-band orchestra without a single electronic instrument and a repertoire comprising purely hits from the swing era sung in Estonian, English, German, Russian and Polish. Their crooner, a tall young guy named Mart Sander, was so perfectly stylish and absolutely cool that I virtually cried with laughter throughout the whole show.

In the middle of the festival on Victory Day (May 9), they launched a huge 'Peace Concert' in one of the town squares. All the Estonian rock stars (Ivo Linna, Gunnar Graps, Silvi Vrait and others) played on a hastily erected wooden stage and as a finale they all got together and stood in a row and sang—in the fashionable Band Aid tradition—a song by Peter Vahi of Vitamin called 'One Rhythm One Melody'. I was basking in the sun near the stage and the view seemed to be very touching. "Nice people, these Estonians," I thought as I listened to 'One Melody'. "They can get on and be friendly . . . I wonder if we could get *our* bitchy rockers together. Why not? If I could find a good cause . . ."

Well, the cause was in the air—in both senses of the word. The Chernobyl tragedy was the talk of the town. Our helplessness and uselessness in this dramatic situation was really upsetting. So . . . what about a big rock concert to help the victims of Chernobyl? The project was launched . . . and immediately on returning to Moscow, on May 13, I rushed to see Alla Pugachova.

This remarkable woman is worthy of further mention; indeed, her career and adventures would make a good theme for an entire book. Since 1975, when Alla, then 26, won a pop contest in Bulgaria with her biggest ever hit 'Harlequin', she has been the biggest star of Soviet pop music thus far. In fact, she alone has changed the face of Soviet pop: after decades dominated by ultra-smooth mannequin-like performers, Alla hit the stage like a fireball with red headed fury, a natural voice, frivolous manners and love problems. The audience was breathless, they fell in love, cried in ecstasy and ran in tears. Pugachova became a social phenomena: a female who became one of the most popular personalities in a country where all the heroes are traditionally strong males—cosmonauts, marshals and politicians.

I have never been a big fan of cabaret pop,* it's just not my cup of tea, but Alla's talent and charisma are undeniable. What's more important is that she's a very interesting personality, far deeper and more inspired than her music suggests. Although she's often accused of being in bad taste by intellectuals, she's not bourgeois at all—rather the opposite. To prove that, here's one little story from the old days.

In the late seventies West German television requested an interview with the Soviet 'superstar' and it was essential for them to arrange it at

*It seems Bette Midler is the closest act to Pugachova in the West. She's also Alla's personal favourite. After seeing *The Rose* on video, she just sighed . . . 'That's me'.

her own home in 'family' surroundings. Pugachova decided she didn't want to meet the foreigners in her small and poor flat on the outskirts of Moscow so she approached a wealthy composer, moved into his place with her little daughter, put on a dressing gown and played the hostess. (The composer's wife acted as the cook!) After a while the trick was revealed and the German TV man was so shocked that he himself started working on providing a new flat for the 'superstar'—and she's still grateful to him. This is the truth behind Alla's now legendary luxurious apartment in Gorky Street.

It was in this very flat that we first sat and discussed the Chernobyl concert project. Alla was for it and after some 'telephone' preparation, we went to the Party Central Committee. For both of us this was our first visit to this place, but Alla didn't have to show her identity card to get in: she was immediately admitted by the stunned guards. Our idea was approved and even more. They said: "We understand that this is the initiative of young musicians, so do it yourselves and in the way that you want to do it. There's no need to make it 'over-organised' and official. If you have any problems, just give us a ring and you will have our support."

The fact that only rock acts were going to perform also met with no objections. Encouraged by this, we asked whether or not we could invite some Western rock stars, like Bruce Springsteen or Sting. The answer was "Why not?" "Maybe invite Michael Jackson," suggested one of the officials politely. There was only one request—and a sensible one at that . . . "Try to produce your concert in a way that won't look like a 'feast in times of plague'."

The idea of inviting foreign guest artists was soon dropped. Here, as opposed to our internal affairs, we could only operate through official channels—the Foreign Ministry and Gosconcert*—and that was a slow train in a situation where we needed a rocket. Time was the key factor and we set a date for the concert as soon as possible—May 30. The venue was the Olympic Stadium, the biggest indoor venue in Moscow, with a capacity of 30,000. This meant that we had only two weeks to arrange everything from scratch.

The same day we started calling the bands. No one asked the usual star questions like 'who else will play' or 'which number on the bill are we'. They all just said OK without further comment. Autograph, Bravo, Cruise, Vladimir Kuzmin, Alexander Gradsky and, naturally, Alla and her band Recital, were all signed in a few hours.

Alla's flat now became the headquarters for what we called the Account 904 Concert (bank account number 904 was opened for cash donations from people who wanted to help the Chernobyl victims) and the following day we got dozens of phone calls from other bands who wanted to participate—but we were forced to refuse as we already had enough acts for one evening. We simply asked others to organise their

*The division of the Ministry Of Culture responsible for foreign tours by Soviet artists and vice versa.

own benefits—it was allowed—or ask a concert hall's administration to place their concert income into the 904 account. This was done by many bands, including Time Machine.

Some arguing between us was inevitable of course. Pugachova loves Hollywood style pomp, so she insisted that the concert should include some circus acts, ballet and theatrics. "It doesn't have to look like a mourning ceremony . . . let them all see we're not down," she said. I was for a more strict approach—no funeral marches but also no carnival. Eventually we agreed on a compromise: only the ballet remained from her suggestions.

I managed to escape for a couple of days to Vilnius for their second rock festival. I brought them a message from Alla Pugachova—it was read from the stage at the opening ceremony—where she passionately asked the rockers of the Soviet Union to join the Account 904 movement and give money to Chernobyl victims, and the organisers did just that. The festival was excellent: Aquarium, Bravo, Sipoli, Aria and the Gunnar Graps Group all played, along with a couple of interesting new bands which I'll tell you about later. I couldn't really enjoy this visit to my beloved city and the great music because my mind was elsewhere. I had realised an aim with this festival and that was that Bravo should become the 'laureates'. For many the participation of this amateur band seemed mysterious, especially since I act as a kind of manager for them and might thus seem to be pushing my own clients into the big league. Frankly speaking, this is probably correct, but I was confident that Zhanna was great anyway.

The event came closer and closer and the tension grew. There were many who didn't sleep much in those two weeks: Yevgeny Boldin (the chief manager), Anatoly Isaenko (scenography), Matvey Anichkin (assistant to the director, i.e. Alla—he's Cruise's manager). The night before the concert we spent at the headquarters and Alla was scared. "Never in my life have I felt such stage fright," she told me. We had no time for a rehearsal because the PA could only be erected a few hours before the event. That night I proposed a toast: "Even if tomorrow's action is a pure failure, we'll still get some money. It's a noble attempt so the people will forgive us." By this time we'd raised about 100,000 roubles through ticket sales and tender hearted Alla had requested that this money go to the needs of the evacuated children. Also we planned to release a double LP and a video of the concert which could earn further sums. (Unfortunately neither of these ideas came to fruition.)

Six hours before the concert something came up that we had been anticipating for a long time. A large crowd of officials from the Ministry Of Culture and various musical departments and concert organisations came to the Olympic Stadium. These were the bureaucrats we had ignored and—because we had ignored them—managed to accomplish what we had. They were frightened and indignant: "Where's the official programme? The censored song lyrics? Permission? Approval? Signatures? Seals? We have received none of these. We are against Gradsky performing. Who the hell are Bravo? We will not allow this concert." We listened to all this noise, and then let them know that we didn't need their permission, that the concert would happen without them. Eventually all these gloomy men and women faded in the doorway murmuring things about being against it and that we were entirely responsible for it ourselves.

For me, this was a tremendous moment, a very rare event in our sad rock history. The courageous will of the artists had triumphed over the bureaucracy. Yet a bitter question arose: did we need an awful tragedy like Chernobyl to make it possible? Or was it that the *perestroika* was really happening? I think it was a question of both factors coming together.

The concert was OK. It was filmed by more than a dozen western TV companies and even Soviet Central TV. We had a direct TV link-up with Kiev, and about 50 workers and soldiers from Chernobyl sat in the Kiev studio watching the gig while we watched them from the stage. Little Zhanna got quite hysterical before her appearance but sang well after all. Gradsky performed a very emotional song about Vladimir Vysotsky ('If he was alive he'd be among us now . . .') and won fierce applause. Valery Gaina amazed the westerners with his guitar tricks. At the end of the show everybody got up on stage and sang a song about friendship . . . under the stadium's high roof white doves flew in the sky.

Musically it could have been far more interesting but this wasn't our main goal. We raised some useful money. We established rock as a positive social force and proved that rockers are not just a doubtful bunch of hooligans but real patriots. We also showed the West that rock really exists in the Soviet Union.

Alla performed beyond her limit, and she had the hardest task of the day. After the gig she was sitting in her dressing room, completely white and barely responding to the compliments. At the artists' exit a vast crowd of fans had gathered. We said our goodbyes. Alla and her escorts left in her old black Mercedes and I left on foot in the opposite direction. As I walked along the street, bag on my shoulder, I could hear the massed army chanting 'Alla Alla' behind me. Alone, I headed for Peace Avenue subway station. It was an emotional moment. I next headed for the Leningrad Railway Station. This year's city rock festival had just begun there.

The Fourth Festival was fun. For the first time they held it not in the poky rock club hall but in the big Nevsky Cultural Palace with a good PA. The whole rock-*tusovka* from different cities were there and they arranged a summit meeting for the whole rock club movement in an attempt to somehow co-ordinate things. The locals complained to me that I hadn't invited them to the Olympic Stadium 904 Concert. "Well," I said. "Springsteen and Gabriel weren't invited, so you're in good company!"

Natasha Veselova, the charming new curator of the rock club, claimed that all their bands were now brave and sharp. I missed Alisa's set where they sang songs like 'Atheist Twist' and 'My Generation' ('My generation bowed its head, My generation is afraid to sing, My generation feels the pain, but puts itself beneath the lash again.') Kino's programme proved that Natasha was right. They started with a song called 'We Want Changes' and continued in the same militant spirit:

> 'We were born in small flats of the new district.
> We lost our virginity in the battles for love.
> The hopes that you gave us
> And the clothes you tailored
> Are now too tight for us
> And now we come to tell you
> It's we who'll act from now on.'

Kino not only played much better but in Viktor Tsoy's songs one could feel a positive enthusiasm and drive rather than alienated sorrow:

> 'And those who are weak, they live from drink to drink
> They cry: "They don't let us sing!"
> They cry: "You just can't sing here!"
> But we are marching—we are strong and full of energy.
> Our frozen fingers strike the matches
> That will light the big fires.'

Perhaps these rock marches are too categorical and too like street posters but they transmitted precisely the spirit of the time and the mood of the crowd: big expectations and renewal of street festivals. I'd never seen so many open smiles in Leningrad; the typical bitter and dark image of rockers was no longer appropriate or cool.

Televisor's performance was the biggest revelation of the festival and, probably, one of the most stunning moments in the history of Soviet rock. The band have changed their line-up and they played quirky syncopated electronic funk that seemed to be the perfect setting for Mikhail Borzykin's nervous escapades. Their set was the most dangerous, the sharpest and most critical:

*A reference to break-dancing.

> 'Tricky kids on asphalt playing West*
> Well they can make some noise.
> Why do tears always fall

But look . . . there behind the column is standing
The same man in a grey suit with a look like concrete.
Dead environment full of living creatures,
Drowning in tusovka, the Crown of Creation
Avant-garde on its knees and greedy sponsors,
And again, humiliation at the wages.
But we're marching, we're marching,
And this match is like stamping in the same place.'

The line 'We're marching' was just like one of Tsoy's songs. In one instant a passionate call to arms, in another an angry question. But I don't think there's a big contradiction: it's like two sides of one coin, two features of one fact, the fact that the real movement has started. The new social climate and the impulse of renewal has provided rockers with new energy and a thirst for responsibility. Those who had something to say weren't afraid of open statements. And they didn't ask for permission or directives before saying it. Borzykin's songs have scared the officials . . . "Well, that's *too* much." He was fighting for a right to be uncompromising, carrying Gorbachev's quotes in his wallet and showing them to scared officials. A song that shook the festival and established Televisor as the most significant rock band around was called 'Get Out Of Control':

'We were watched from the days of kindergarten.
Some nice men and kind women
Beat us up. They chose the most painful places
And treated us like animals on the farm.
So we grew up like a disciplined herd.
We sing what they want and live how they want.
And we look at them downside up as if we're trapped.
We just watch how they hit us.
Get out of control.
Get out of control.
And sing what you want.
And not just what is allowed.
We have a right to yell.'

Against messages like this Aquarium looked insufficient, like last year's thing. They now preached nice nostalgic folk rock with spiritual lyrics (a typical title is 'Love Is All We Are'). Zoo added a vocal trio to their regular line-up and performed some soft core satirical songs in a back-to-the-roots r'n'b manner. Strange Games have split into two bands: The Games (Sollogub brothers plus a sharp new guitarist) played intensive yet monotonous post punk, while AVIA (keyboard player, saxophonist and percussion from Strange Games) showed an amusing synthesis of kitschy pop tunes, jazz rock and musical extravaganza. Both bands were pretty good and promising and AVIA in particular were funny and unusual.

Of the all new bands I liked the punkish Object Of Mockery led by an acrobatic lead singer nicknamed Ricochet, and Auction, a ska/new wave showband whose grotesque looking frontman, nicknamed Spitball, unpacked rolls of toilet paper while crying "Money is paper". It was clear that Moscow's belief that they had left Leningrad rock behind was just not true. It was probably true that the capital's best bands—Zvuki Mu, Centre and Copernicus—sounded more original and Russian-like, but they were only three. As for Bravo . . . they joined the professional army in June which wasn't necessarily catastrophic but rather sad (albeit inevitable).

There was a remarkable appendix to the Leningrad Festival. The day after its conclusion Billy Bragg came to town. This wonderful punk-bard had performed at a political rock event in Helsinki and had asked the Finns to arrange a small tour for him and manager Pete Jenner.* So we had three days of chatting, meetings and soulful sleepless sessions in the white night.

Aside from the discussion with Billy, we dared to organise a real concert—at the Komsomol City Committee!!—and the whole exotic rock club crowd came, probably for the first time in their lives. Billy sang, spoke and answered some questions like, "Do you really believe in the Trade Unions and such rubbish?" He was suddenly confronted with the challenge of supporting and enforcing working class ideals among sceptical red rockers. He showed the audience British made t-shirts with Yuri Gagarin and Mayakovsky designs on them and he told his audience: "Many artists and musicians and young people in the West now turn to the revolutionary arts of Soviet Russia in search of new ideas and new styles. So you don't have to look to the West for inspiration. We've got no answers to your problems. You've got a tremendous cultural heritage, so why not stick to your own roots and develop the avant-garde art achievements of the twenties?" I had the honour of translating Billy's speech for the audience. Hopefully, thanks to Billy, our kids will change their minds about certain things.

Another important event in June was the release in the US of a double album called 'The Red Wave'. The record, featuring material by Aquarium, Kino, Alisa and Strange Games, was compiled by an energetic young Californian named Joanna Stingray. The album was the culmination of a long story: Miss Stingray, an ambitious amateur rock singer herself, first came to Leningrad in the autumn of 1984 and then returned many times, making friends with many rock club musicians and arriving at the centre of *tusovka*. This rich child of Beverly Hills had found a new and challenging Disneyland for herself but her intentions were serious. She has recorded English language versions of

*Actually, this wasn't the first informal contact of this kind. In December 1985 Chris Cross from Ultravox arrived in Leningrad and even played a gig with Popular Mechanics in the rock club.

128

Grebenschikov, Tsoy and Kinchev's songs and, eventually, realised the Red Wave project.

For us there was nothing new on this record (except the cover). It was compiled from recordings made between 1982 and 1985 and released here on cassettes. Also, all the songs on the LP had passed the censor years before. But it was the West's first real opportunity to learn something about current Soviet rock.* It was quite amazing that Joanna had to smuggle the tapes out and violate the copyright laws.

When I asked her why she didn't do it in a legal way and avoid risks for herself and the musicians, she replied: "Do you really think the officials would allow it?" In 1986 why not, I thought. But of course there is always cause for pessimism as well.

It must be said that the official Soviet institutions have never done anything to help the export and international promotion of Soviet rock music. They've created lots of artificial barriers which are illogical and contrary to their own commercial interests. Even when the initial interest has been shown by the West they have said 'nyet'.

An example occurred in the spring of 1985 when representatives of London's Capital Radio came to Moscow in the hope of signing up some Soviet rock acts for their annual festival. They were especially interested in two bands, Time Machine and Arsenal, whom they had heard of in the UK. So they asked Gosconcert to introduce them to these two bands. The answer they received implied that Time Machine had split up many years ago and Arsenal were "touring Outer Mongolia" and were thus uncontactable. In reality Makarevich's group were alive and well while Arsenal were at that time ensconced in Moscow, not even in Kiev or Novosibirsk. Then I served as a guide and, quite realistically, recommended Autograph and Rock-Atelier, both officially approved bands with some international (Soviet-bloc) experience. But even with them the arrangements just became drowned in a sea of bureaucracy. A few months later Autograph played a couple of songs in the Moscow TV studios and this was the total Soviet contribution to Bob Geldof's Live Aid project.

The jealousy and conspiracy of silence promoted by the official organs only served to arouse the curiosity of the Western media, and the forbidden fruit of Soviet rock received more and more speculative attention. In 1985 and 1986 there were dozens of articles in French, German, British and American magazines. Several films were also made, of which a French one called *Rock Around The Kremlin* and the episode about Sergey Kuryokhin from the BBC Comrades programme were the most significant. All these works were very different in approach: analytical or sensational, ironical or sympathetic, realistic or fictitious, but everywhere the information was somehow one-sided. There were the same characters and the same faces in all the articles, so the general picture was far from objective.

*Two other LPs, a Time Machine album and a compilation of Latvian underground bands (including Yellow Postmen) were issued before that but they were released on tiny labels and aroused no international interest.

For example, some useless members of the Leningrad *tusovka* received more coverage than all the Moscow amateur bands put together. Stas Namin, Boris Grebenschikov and even Alla Pugachova were hailed as originators of Soviet rock, and Popular Mechanics were proclaimed a new spiritual youth movement, integrating the whole of Leningrad rock led by a guru called Kuryokhin. I'm not being fiendish or even accusing my foreign colleagues of being inaccurate in their twisted vision of our rock scene . . . in fact, they just reflected what they were shown or told about and, as some people here have more contacts and a stronger will to promote themselves, so those people enjoyed greater coverage while other (no less interesting) bands like Zoo or Televisor or Centre or bands from the Baltic Republic, just stayed in the shade.

The rock export situation started to change slowly after 1986. The Stas Namin Group* went to the USA, West Germany and Japan (where they played a Tokyo Festival alongside Peter Gabriel, Lou Reed and Howard Jones, among others); Autograph toured France and visited Austria and Denmark; Dialogue performed at the MIDEM Festival in Cannes. Capital Radio finally succeeded, after two years of trying, in bringing Autograph and Dialogue to London for their festival in July 1987. Press reviews in the West were generally favourable but it's too early to talk about any real breakthrough into the new Western market since most of these encounters were like 'peace and friendship' missions and not actual commercial tours. There are still no record deals, although I've heard that Stas Namin has signed a contract with CBS.

The new winds have also blown away some thick dust from the Melodia shelves and mixing boards. They have released the first 'official' albums by Autograph (in the band's seventh year of existence), Aquarium (15th year) and Time Machine (19th year). In the pipeline are albums by younger groups like Bravo, Cruise, Forum and Secret. * Also worth mentioning is the long awaited official release of Beatles material (songs from 1963 and 1964) as well as licensed albums by Dire Straits, The Alan Parsons Project and Whitney Houston. These releases, of course, will not have any effect on the black market for records, where the prices remain at the same level of around 50 roubles per disc.

Enough of the formal information . . . the most important and lively things were happening elsewhere, which reflects the all-round importance of *tusovka*. In the streets there emerged crowds of bizarrely dressed young people who were no longer afraid of being arrested for their spiky coloured hair, rough clothes or metal chains. They all belonged to various so-called 'informal youth groups' and passionately aimed to expose their particular style. The *'metallisti'* (teenage followers of heavy metal) scared citizens with their black leather suits, bracelets with iron studs and amulets in the skull and cross-bones style. The *'breikeri'* (break dance fans) hung around in sporty American-looking clothes with ghetto blasters on their shoulders. Then there was a hippie revival (now they

*The Stas Namin Group have a well deserved reputation for pop rather than rock but lately, and especially with foreign touring, they've hardened and sharpened their act and now sound more like an American AOR band.

*Forum play melodic teeny-bopper electro-pop, featuring Viktor Saltykov, the former Manufactura singer. Secret are a Leningrad quartet who accurately imitate the style of the early Beatles with Russian lyrics. They also play a couple of Mike Naumenko songs.

130

called themselves simply 'The System') of people who wore bands on their foreheads, dirty jeans, saris and beads, and listened to sixties music, Aquarium and Crematorium. The fact that the neo-hippies don't differ at all from the same 'System' of 15 years ago doesn't disturb them one iota: they claim they stand for eternal ideals.

The long haired and bearded young Russophiles look almost like the hippies but they don't listen to rock'n'roll but take part in the restoration of old churches and other ancient relics. Who else? . . . Well, the new stilyagi in baggy suits and stiletto heels rush to concerts by Bravo and Mister Twister (a new Moscow rockabilly band) while our New Romantics, loaded with cheap *bijouterie*, languidly listen to N. Copernicus and Night Avenue. The radical bohemians wear tall soldier boots and the clothes of the opposite sex; they had no band of their own until recently when there emerged one called The Central Russian Height (a pun which may be taken as a geographical area or the Average Russian's sublimity!), a bunch of musically inept but outrageous avant-garde painters. They make much fun with songs like 'House Of Stalin', 'Spaceship Heroes' and 'Born In The USSR'.

Finally, all the advanced youth groups now have their own mutual enemy in the form of the so-called *luberi*. The *luberi* are young boys from industrial towns in the Moscow suburbs, not rich and poorly informed and thus tortured by an inferiority complex when faced with the fashionable and cosmopolitan downtown crowd. So the working class kids decided to overcome their inferiority complexes by body-building, getting together in gangs and beating up anyone whose appearance they didn't like. Their attitude is also influenced by Russian nationalism—as an alternative to the Westernised rich kids—so a parallel between the *luberi* and the British skinhead movement can easily be drawn. The only big difference is the fact that the *luberi* don't have their own music and, in fact, are ignorant in this area. The conflict between the *luberi* and others grew to a dramatic scale in the winter of 1986/7 when there were well organised fights (shades of Mods v Rockers!) with hundreds of people involved.

Unlike in the bad old days, all this mess is widely covered and commented on in the press. As the authorities now demand a socially conscious and 'critical' approach from the mass media and are no longer afraid of sensationalism, the 'informal youth groups' became darlings of the media, alongside the pioneers of private enterprise and the exposure of corrupt old-regime bureaucrats. Usually such articles started with an angry letter from some *babooshka** or working class veteran complaining about current youth trends, or with a description of a *metallisti* bunker/infernal disco/hippies' den, followed by an interview with some young outsiders from which it was possible to glean that they were not rotten to the core but simply expressed a wish to differ from the masses (which is no longer considered a deadly sin). The articles

*An old traditional woman, or grandmother.

131

would finish on a moral tone, suggesting that the movement should not be banned but that the kids should be helped and organised. All quite superficial but nice nonetheless. For the first time in my life I've witnessed 'alternative' youth carefully reading the 'official' newspapers. The press also made some good points in criticising the traditionally nasty attitude towards kids at concerts. After the UB40 tour, when the militiamen stopped the audience from dancing in the hall and pushed them back in their seats, there were several angry reviews that condemned the guards and asked whether it really was dangerous to dance during such performances. Thus *glasnost* disturbed the conservative rules—a good thing, too.

There was also a flood of articles about domestic rock and almost all of them were very favourable. Ageing composers, komsomol chiefs and cultural functionaries all now decided that rock was of significance after all. "Yes, this is interesting. This is new!(?) This is what youth needs!" The most self-critical of these were even repentant. "We've recognised rock too late," they said. "We've treated rock with the wrong methods."

The campaign around Aquarium was especially pompous. Boris' group had all the necessary attributes to become the year's heroes: talent, intellect, popularity, a martyrized past and a safe present. After their one-and-a-half hour programme was shown on Central TV on a Saturday night, I received several telephone calls from my mother's ageing and respectable acquaintants. "Oh, what nice intelligent people your friends are," they said. "They are totally unlike all that vulgar pop."

Hey Boris . . . is this what you expected? "I don't want to follow Makarevich's path, that would be too banal, but what can I do? And what can't I do?" Boris told me while waving goodbye to another correspondent from a central paper. "I feel that I'm being used and I definitely don't like it. I'm ready to get angry but I just can't. Please . . . make me angry about something."

I think there are still many reasons to be angry. We now have a very tense struggle between old and new trends in the country, and thousands of problems remain unsolved. This also applies to the state of rock. Even in the noisy pro-rock campaign one can detect lots of insincerity and demagogy. Conformists and monsters, the people who accused rock of being a form of 'musical alcoholism' or a 'creature of the CIA' are now eager to jump on the rock bandwagon. They keep doing their dirty work, like writing articles blaming Joanna Stingray for vicious piracy while apparently defending the rights of the good but 'cheated' Soviet rockers. The rotten old spirit is changing its colours to follow the new fashion, and it is still dangerous.

Then there's still the old disease of using many loud words yet being frightened to undertake any real changes. After lots of speeches there is still no rock magazine in the USSR, no new record labels which could serve as a constructive alternative to the flabby Melodia, and no union for rockers like the Composers' Union.

On the subject of the latter, the conservative pop, the Russian Tin Pan Alley if you like, is alive and well and far from surrendering its position on the top. In November 1986 there appeared on TV a brief satirical rock programme called *The Funny Boys* which promoted the view that since the younger generation need (and have!) their own music there was no need to impose the eternal cliches of Soviet easy listening music on them. The programme was heavily criticised for 'putting the wedge between the generations' and wasn't shown again which is against the general rule. During another TV programme Centre performed 'The Useless Song', a harsh verdict on Soviet mass produced pop:

> 'The useless song—head is empty.
> Useless song—the words are simple.
> Useless song—but you can dance to it.
> Useless song—doesn't disturb your sleep.
> Useless song—a gloomy event.
> Useless song—a stop in the development.
> Useless song—a creative impotence.
> Useless song—spiritual disability.'

This number was eventually excluded from the programme.

This is not necessarily the well-known syndrome of 'one step forward and two steps back' but an indication of the fact that the fight is on and it's too early to declare the fall of cultural bureaucracy.

Zvuki Mu came up with the biggest unofficial 'hit' of the season, a song called 'Soyuzpechat' (The Soviet Press), a piece reflecting the *perestroika* of personality:

> 'I often sit in sadness.
> I can cry without tears.
> I just make my eyes empty.
> And say "I'm for it"
> To every question
> But in the morning
> On the way past the news-stand
> I often want what I don't have.
> I was taught to dream
> By the fresh print of newspapers
> By the Soviet press.'

In the last verse the doomed state of mind of the hero is transformed:

> 'When you pass me by
> Don't make a face at me

As if you never care.
What the country will say about us
What the Soviet press will print.'

OK . . . one of the main dogmas of socialist realism is to show a person in his dialectical revolutionary development (as in Gorky's novel, *The Mother*) . . . so here it is.

I shook my old memories by playing lead guitar with Zvuki Mu at the first anniversary of the Moscow Rock Lab concert. The show ended up in an unprecedented orgy: Peter Mamonov was lying on stage while some girls in the audience (including his own wife) licked his black patent leather shoes. Earlier, a hysterical blues band called Polite Refusal threw pieces of raw meat into the audience while they were playing!

The opening of the new season at the Leningrad rock club was no less wild. Auction played a new set entitled 'All Is Quiet In Baghdad' (they could have said Kabul, incidentally) which included a 'belly dance' number (at one of their later concerts they performed an actual striptease). The Games sang their new hit anthem with an endless chorus of . . . 'Nothing is beloved, nothing is sacred'. Televisor finished their set with a passionate version of John Lennon's 'Revolution'. Aquarium started their performance by demanding that the *druzhinniky** leave the hall and then performed a 20 minute chant of a reggae song called 'Babylon' ('In this city there must be someone alive') during which the whole audience stood on their chairs. The well disciplined rock community had started to dig the taste of freedom.

*That night the druzhinsky (volunteer police helpers) arrested some musicians in the rock club and started a conflict with the administration which the rockers eventually won— surprise, surprise!

Kino performed a concert the day after the Reagan/Gorbachev summit in Iceland. Unfortunately our leaders couldn't make a deal in Reykjavik but here, on a rock stage . . . "Russians and Americans can easily agree and collaborate with each other," said Viktor Tsoy as he introduced Joanna Stingray to the audience. They performed a bilingual song with the American chanting, 'Feel so good, feel so right, hold me tight, kiss me once, kiss me twice, feels so nice. Give me some more of your love,' while the Russian text was less straightforward (which is typical when comparing Russian and Western lyrics):

'You feel the waves, soft waves behind you
Stand up as there's no one else to save you.'

There is just one big failure in Moscow and Leningrad's great rock Babylon. Very few good new bands emerge from this great mess. It almost looks like the goldmine is exhausted. More promising is the rejuvenation of the rock scene in the provinces. Since the experience of the pioneering rock clubs was approved officially as a positive achievement, similar associations emerged in every major city where there was a trace of interest in rock. Now we have rock clubs in Sverdlovsk,

Novosibirsk, Odessa, Vilnius, Tallin, Minsk, Yaroslavl, Vladivostok and more, about 20 in all. (There's still nothing in central Asia.) I travelled from one local festival to another and among hundreds of unknown and mostly very boring bands I found some real gems.

First there's Antis (which means 'duck' in Lietuvian), a fantastic band and my real discovery of 1986. They played on the same bill as Zvuki Mu at the opening concert of the Vilnius rock club and gave Moscow's biggest attraction a distinctly hard time. They comprise several young architects with wild imaginations supported by some fine semi-pro jazz players. Their leader, Algis Kauspedas, is two metres tall, quite charming and a monster-lover who looks like a sophisticated Count Dracula. He's carried on stage in a coffin and sings into a telephone and their surreal show goes on in this manner accompanied by hard driving mutant rhythm'n'blues. Their tough and satirical lyrics are a tough test for *glasnost*: one song, about two lovers who are always trying to get the top position when making love, is considered to be an allegory of Soviet/American relations. Then there is a song about a certain leader whose main activity is to get more and more medals (guess who?) as well as many other intriguing items. "We are called a 'Gorbachev' band in Lietuvania," claims Algis.

Then there is 003, a neurotic PIL-like band from Kaliningrad who have unfortunately split up; Ironix, a young poetess from Gorky called Marina Kulakova who reads rap poetry to a computer pulse; Kalinov Bridge from Novosibirsk who play heavy blues which somehow remind me of pagan Slavic songs; Nautilus (Sverdlovsk), a classy electronic new wave band with some of the most socially painful lyrics I've ever heard . . . the long awaited and much desired signs of life in Russia. I was always sort of hypnotised and intrigued by the huge dimensions of my own country and thought to myself that if they have electricity they must have rock there. Since childhood I remember a classic Soviet painting—V. I. Lenin At The Plan of Electrification—in which the leader of the revolution looks at a giant map with many tiny lights on it. As I write this the picture comes to mind.

So, here I am in the especially cold winter of 1987. We have just had a party plenum which confirmed the new line on democratisation. A friend of mine published an article in *Pravda* entitled 'Let's Have Fun'. Yet Gosconcert is afraid to bring Cyndi Lauper for a tour. There are queues at the cinemas where they show a film entitled *Is It Easy To Be Young*, a shockingly brave and clever movie by Juris Podnieks (my former TV partner on the Latvian TV Video-Ritmi programme) which shows a true picture of Soviet 'problem youth' from punks to Afghan veterans. The rock laboratories have been given formal status as state commercial organisations and will soon make The Festival Of Hope in which a new punk band Ghudo-Yudo will perform a censored song entitled 'Sex Revolution Is What The Country Needs'. Yoko Ono is coming for another Peace Congress (I wonder if Kolya Vasin will see her). Jungle and Yellow Postmen were invited to the Alternative Music Festival in Warsaw . . . eventually Postmen went but Jungle were replaced with the even more alternative Time Machine. Some things don't ever change . . . like the Central TV which is still boring. Alla Pugachova attended the San Remo Festival, and sang with one Barry Manilow in Vienna. Alexander Gradsky was elected president of the Moscow Rock Club (as opposed to Rock Lab—this one is mostly for professionals). Aquarium were invited to the USA to record an album with some superstars. Let's keep our fingers crossed. Meanwhile, they've just written a good song called 'Fly, Babooshkas, Fly'.

> *'So many babooshkas, and each one wears a tie*
> *Why do you have such big ears, babooshkas?*
> *Why do you have such big teeth, babooshkas?*
> *Thanks, babooshkas, for coming to listen to us . . .*
> *Our life is simple, but there's something in it we can't*
>   *understand,*
> *Like a head served up on a plate.*
> *Why does the game always have only one goalpost?*
> *And why are there always so many umpires on the field?*
> *Excuse us, babooshkas, we are very tired of you.*
> *Go and find somewhere else and a proper job to do,*
> *And we will quietly sigh and wipe away a tear*
> *And wave you all bye-bye, waving white handkerchiefs.*
> *Farewell, babooshkas, your aim was always dead-on target.*
> *Farewell, babooshkas, your looks quenched all the flames*
> *Farewell, babooshkas, although you are always near the*
>   *doors.*
> *But whoever told you that you have the right to rule us?*
> *A flock of babooshkas flies through the night sky*
> *Fly, darlings, fly away.'*

I believe that the fading 'grannies' will never fly back. And this would mean that we all, and also Soviet rock, are stepping into a brand new phase. So, one chapter of history is now over and my account of it is finished. Thank you.

AFTERWORD

Right now the rock music situation in the USSR is more complex and contradictory than ever before. After a strictly black-and-white balance of power during the years of prohibition, all our old stereotypes are obsolete now thanks to glasnost and the economic *perestroika*. There are more opportunities available to rock musicians, but it's harder for some to get orientated in the new situation. And not all manifestations of the new democratisation necessarily favour rock; the genre is still controversial and vulnerable.

This spring witnessed the biggest anti-rock backlash of the past couple of years. It was initiated by some Russophile writers, supported by certain officials in the Ministry Of Culture and the central television networks, and featured active agitation by the so-called Memory group, a chauvinistic organisation that carries on anti-semitic propaganda and decrees rock music as 'satanic'. All this under the banner of glasnost.

The backlash reflected more than just the personal tastes of those involved; it also spoke of an attitude towards rock that exists among some major ideologists and can be summarised as follows: We won't ban rock, as was mistakenly done before, but we won't encourage it either, because we believe that rock is harmful to Soviet youth. As a result of the spring campaign, the second annual Rock Panorama, which was to have been the biggest Soviet rock festival ever, was postponed from April until December, 1987. Other festivals, though, went as scheduled and were big successes.

In such a fluid situation, the only factor that can work for rock to guarantee its further legal development is economics. Rock continues to sell, and this makes it valuable to state cultural agencies switched under the new economic reforms to cost accounting and self-financing. Take the Melodia label, for instance: until recently they could bury record stores under tons of records that didn't sell (Brezhnev speeches or balalaika ensembles) and still feel fine, because their operation was subsidised. Now, if they don't want to go bankrupt, they must release things that people really want. Incidentally, Melodia's planned releases for 1987 include more rock titles than for the entire preceding decade.

Next, both the philharmonias and rock clubs are also switching to cost accounting and self-financing. This means the demise of the underground, since 'amateur' bands will now start signing record contracts and making money from their gigs. We've waited a long time for this, and it's a great day, but . . . previously, musicians exercised their creativity under the slogan 'We've Got Nothing To Lose', and thus didn't think much about altering their work to accommodate the censors or win official prestige. Now, whether they recognise it consciously or not, the new conditions push them towards compromise, and one can already see some effects. There are suddenly far more purely commercial rock bands, and noticeably fewer home-made cassettes.

This is just one of several paradoxes of *perestroika*, and I'm not going to get melodramatic or try to stir up nostalgia for the nasty old times by arguing that the worse the official attitude towards rock, the better the rock music that comes out. But think about this: I don't consider that glasnost is demagogy; otherwise how could the infamous Swine perform before 1,500 people at this year's Leningrad festival? Or how could the censors pass the lyrics to Televisor's latest hit, called 'My Father Is A Fascist'? In fact, our problem is just the opposite: too few rock bands dare to test glasnost. It's a stunning fact but true—there are articles in the central press every day that seem more courageous and more angry than the songs of our radical rockers! And this is sad. It seems that the long-awaited sunlight has blinded most of the creatures crawling out of the underground.

Yes, rock is no longer the challenge to society that it once was, and soon we'll probably have a real showbiz infrastructure with hit parades and gold records. Which is OK, because I'm confident that our rock will endure these pleasures and temptations and maintain its non-conformist spirit, just as it has survived the decades of trauma and some decidedly indelicate treatment. Zvuki Mu have a good line on the subject:

'After all that's happened,
I feel like a rescued skydiver.'

The future is bright and unpredictable. Nothing scares us now.

APPENDIX I

SELECTED RECORDINGS

All recordings released on the official Melodia label unless otherwise noted.

Each listing is followed by a year of release, though many of the recordings were made between one and four years before the record became available commercially.

Antis

Antis (1987)

Probably the finest Soviet 'official' rock LP recorded to date. Crazy vocals, catchy tunes and a thick brass sound. Their second album, recorded recently in Warsaw, is in the pipeline.

Apelsin

Apelsin I (1979)

Apelsin II (1981)

Estonian country rock and parody band who also played on the LP 'Cuckoo' (1977) by the vocal group Collage.

Aquarium

Aquarium (1987)

The songs are taken from two cassette albums, 'Day Of The Silver' and 'December Children', without remixing. Sleeve notes are by the famous poet Andrei Voznesensky.

Equinox (1988)

Their first recording, made specially for official release in Melodia's Leningrad studios. Very polished.

Arax

The Confession (1983)

The veteran Moscow band creates a 'Pinkfloydesque' background to poet Yevgeny Yevtushenko who narrates his own poetry. The music is written by Gleb May.

Argo

Discophonia (1981)

The Burial (1982)

Light (1983)

Land L (1986)

Lietuvian electronic keyboard band whose music ranges from pipe organ classics and ethnic to computer music.

Arsenal

Arsenal (1979)
Hand-Made (1983)
Second Wind (1985)
Pulse 3 (1986)
   The first two LPs are typical fusion music, the last two instrumental computer/dance material.

Edward Artemiev

The Mood Pictures (1984)
Ode To A Good Messenger (1985)
The Heat Of The Earth (1986)
   More electronic music, this time from the man who's made the soundtracks for most of Andrey Tarkovsky's films. Performed by the Boomerang studio band with some guest vocalists. Some of the Artemiev/Boomerang collaborations are also included in the electronic music compilation 'Metamorphoses' (1981).

Autograph

Autograph (1986)
   A compilation of studio recordings made between 1982 and 1984.

Bioconstructor

Dances on Video (1987)
   A 'serious' synthesizer new wave band from Moscow's Rock Lab.

Black Coffee

Trespass The Threshold (1987)
   The first Soviet heavy metal album displaying all the gimmicks of the genre—from 'gothic' sleeve to song titles like 'Devil In The Flesh'. A best seller.

Boomerang

Boomerang (1982)
Ornament (1984)
   No relation to the Moscow synth band (see Edward Artemiev). This is quite interesting jazz rock from Kazakhstan with some oriental flavour.

Bravo

Bravo (1987)
   From thirties swing to futuristic: mostly old songs plus three more recent numbers, all newly recorded at Time Machine's 8-track studio.
Bravo (1988, Polarvox Records, Finland)
   A Finnish remix of their first Melodia LP which sounds far better than the original.

Brigada S

Brigada S (1987)
   Very entertaining boogie/ska band destined for success. Recording made in Stas Namin's 16-track studio. A must for Melodia.

Carnival

The Steps (1985)
   A pop/rock alliance between singer Alexander Barykin and name composer David Tukhmanov. Guest artists include Valery Gaina from Cruise on lead guitar.

Vladimir Chekasin

Exercises (Leo Records, 1983)
   Among dozens of records of Soviet avant-garde jazz released by this small British indie label, this example is perhaps closer to rock. The best Soviet sax player is accompanied here by Sergey Kuryokhin and Boris Grebenschikov.
Nomen Nescio (1987)
   Eclectic sax-drums-keyboards trip from disco to classical.

Yuri Chernavsky

Automatic Set or The Dreams Repair Camping (1987)
   Fully remixed versions of songs from a 1985 cassette plus new material. Now approved as a soundtrack for a science fiction play.
   New album planned for 1988.

Credo

Our Long Way (1985)
The Yell (1986)
   Latvian hard rock. The latter LP is a suite about Hiroshima.

Cruise

Cruise (1987)
   Ritchie Blackmore meets Cozy Powell and tries to sing in Russian.

DDT

Getting Warmer (1987)

Dialogue

Just So (1985)
Night Rain (1986)
   Artsy dance music from a Siberian based band. Not unlike latter-day Genesis.

Alexander Gradsky

The Lovers Romance (Andrei Konchalovsky film soundtrack, 1976)
Russian Songs (1980)

La Vie Immediate (1984)
The Stadium (rock opera, 1985)
Star Of The Fields (1986)
Satires (1987)

'Russian Songs' is an amazing interpretation of old ethnic material. The all star line-up on The Stadium includes, among other vocalists, Alla Pugachova and Andrei Makarevich. Other LPs are mostly sensitive rock ballads.

Sven Grunberg

Breathe (1981)

Two meditative compositions, one per side, performed on synthesizer and church organ.

New LP expected soon.

Gunesh

I See The Land (1984)

Central Asian fusion music featuring a great drummer and lots of exotic instruments.

Hard Day

Acquiring The Ground (1987)

A non-professional heavy metal band with a huge following in Moscow.

Horizon

Summer City (1986)

An interesting amateur art rock band from the banks of the Volga, favourites of Yuri Saulsky.

In Spe

In Spe I (1983)
In Spe II (1985)

Estonian medieval rock on I, transformed into something avant-garde on II. Side one of the latter album is entitled 'Concerto For The Typewriter'.

Karavan

Karavan (1986)
    Competent Estonian pop/rock.
Karavan II (1987)

Kaseke

Kaseke (1983)

Not exactly fusion, rather instrumental rock music. Very good guitar playing from the guys who used to be in Propeller, the first Estonian punk band.

Vladimir Kuzmin

My Love (1987)
    Our answer to Nik Kershaw (or Stephen Duffy).

142

Livi

The City Of My Fantasy (1986)
> More Latvian hard rock, this time slightly more original than Credo.

Magnetic Band

Roses For Daddy (1982)
> Estonian hard rock plus some blues and reggae. Awful cover.
> Second LP to be released in 1988 under the new name of The Gunnar Graps Group.

Morning

The Process (1987)
> A remarkable avant-rock band from Kharkov in the Ukraine; 'gothic' post-punk meets American minimalism.

Moscow

UFO (1982)
> A studio band performing David Tukhmanov's songs written in the 'progressive rock' manner.

Mosaic

Rubycon (1987)
> During its 20-year existence this semi-pro Moscow band failed to create anything really impressive—a pale shadow of Time Machine.

Music-Seif

Tynis Magi & Music Seif (1983)
> Estonian soul/blues music. Nice warm vocals from Tynis Magi, probably the most heavyweight man in Soviet rock.

Myths

Mythology (1987)

Stas Namin Group

Girl From New York (tentative title, 1987)
> The fifth album from this band and their first attempt to play real rock. The title song is probably based on the band's experiences during their US tour accompanying the Peach Child choir.

Picnic

Hieroglyph (1987)
> A non-remixed version of an 'unofficial' tape released one year before.

Polite Refusal

Dust On My Boots (1988)
> Interesting ethnic influenced Russian singing.

Popular Mechanics

An Introduction to PM (Leo, 1987)
Insect Culture (Ark Records, UK, 1987)
Father and Son (What's So Funny About West Germany, 1987)
   The first LP is a live recording from 1987 and the third is live from Riga. The second is mostly new composers' tape tricks with some additional keyboards from Sergey Kuryokhin.

Alla Pugachova

How Uneasy Is This Road (1982)
I Come To Speak To You (1987)
   My two favourite records from this lady's vast catalogue. Not 100 percent rock but less slick than Barbra Streisand. Avoid the Swedish (English sung) album called 'Watch Out'—it's really bad.

Radar

Trophy (1985)
Baltic Shore (1987)
   Technocratic jazz rock from Estonia's top instrumentalists.

Remix

Night House (1987)
Rodrigo Fomins & Remix (1987)
   Two Latvian session men play instrumental 'cocktail' rock on the first LP and accompany young ex-Livi Rod Stewart sound alike singer on the second.

Rock Hotel

Rock Hotel I (1981)
Ivo Linna & Rock Hotel (1983)
Rock Hotel II (1986)
   Traditional rock'n'roll sung in Estonian—lots of cover versions.

Ruya

Ruya (1982)
   Estonian mainstream rock at its best; energetic and inspired. One of the songs is dedicated to John Lennon and is sung in English.
Rolling Stone (1987)
   Worse than the first one.

Alexey Rybnikov

Juno And Avos (rock opera, 1982)
   A good quality soundtrack from the premier Soviet rock musical; with choir and orchestra.

Secret

Secret (1987)

A Leningrad quartet (formerly members of the Rock Club) imitating the style and sound of the early Beatles. Includes cover versions of two songs by Mike Naumenko. Produced by Time Machine's bass player Alexander Kutikov.

Sipoli

Sipoli (1987)

More pop than their early material, yet quite an interesting LP. Released after Martin Brauns left the band.

Synopsis

Synopsis (1985)

A keyboard-guitar duet featuring Igor Garshnek (Ruya's new leader) and Nevill Blumberg (ex-Radar). More interesting than one would have expected.

Televisor

The Motherland Of Illusions (1988)

Features 'Our Dad Is A Fascist' and other 'glasnost-era' masterpieces, but some still prefer the live recordings.

Time Machine

Hunters For Success (Kismet Records, USA, c1981)
Good Luck! (1986)
Rivers And Bridges (1987)
Ten Years Later (1987)

The American record is an illegal compilation of some studio and concert recordings of horrible quality. The re-recorded versions of some 'classic' TM songs may be found on 'Ten Years Later'. The second and third LPs represent the state of the band today.

David Tukhmanov

How Beautiful Is This World (1973)
In The Wake Of My Memory (1976)

Legendary pop albums of the seventies. At the time they were considered by many to be rock.

Vitamin

Vitamin I (1983)
Vitamin II (1989)

An eclectic but quite funny mixture of pop hits, rock'n'roll and musical parodies. Made—of course—in Estonia.

Vitamin III (1987)

Silvi Vrait
Silvi Vrait (1986)

   Estonia again. Some pop/blues from a lady who enjoys singing Janis Joplin's 'Mercedes Benz' in concert.

Yellow Postmen
Nights (1987)

Zodiac
Disco Alliance (1980)
Music In The Universe (1982)
Music From Films (1985)

   Latvian studio band specialising in instrumental disco music. They have deteriorated from album to album.

SAMPLERS

If you still can't get enough of Estonian rock, then you could try the annual samplers 'Eesti Pop' volumes one to seven. There are lots of recordings from the Tartu Festival, and even one song from Totu Kool—but no Peter Volkonski, of course.

   Some of the top Latvian bands, including Sipoli at their safest, are represented on this republic's similar annual compilations called 'Mikrofons' ('81,'82 etc.) but again no Yellow Postmen or other Riga Rock Club bands.

   On an album called 'Vilnius Pop Groups (1987)' you can find Catharsis on one side and Pulkauskas Group on the other, two modern Lietuvian bands who sound like Tangerine Dream and Men At Work respectively.

   Some of Moscow's rock acts (Bravo, Cruise, Time Machine, Sergey Sarychev, Yuri Loza, etc.) may be heard on two samplers—'Panorama 86' volumes I and II (both 1987), which are partly studio and partly concert recordings from the Rock Panorama 86 Festival.

   Last but not least come two historical compilation double albums: 'Red Wave' (Big Time Records, USA, 1986) featuring one side each from Aquarium, Kino, Alisa and Strange Games; and 'Spring Rhythms Tbilisi-80' (1981) with Time Machine, Autograph, Magnetic Band, Gunesh and others, but no Aquarium.

   'Rocking Soviet' (Antenna, France, 1988) portrays the 'cutting edge of Soviet underground'. Lots of DK plus some Televisor, Kino, Centre, Kalinov Bridge and Cloud Area. The lyric sheet provided is absolutely essential.

STOP PRESS

Sipoli are currently recording their second LP 'Mawgly' (a rock opera). Their first album, once scheduled for release in 1986, is still unavailable due to its unsuitable sleeve, according to officials at Melodia.

   Two compilation LPs of Leningrad rock club bands (including Jungle, AVIA and Televisor) are due to be released soon on Melodia. Upcoming vinyl releases of old and famous 'unofficial' tapes include LPs by Zoo ('White Line'), Alisa ('Energy') and Aquarium ('Radio Africa').

146

APPENDIX II

CASSETTES

There are hundreds of self-made cassette albums in circulation, so this listing is very selective. I've included the cassettes which are the most important (in my opinion) and most popular. I do not include albums whose reference to rock is doubtful (bards, disco, pop), most of the live 'bootlegs' and recordings of especially low quality.

Alisa

Energy (1985)
   Recorded on 8-track in A. Tropillo's studio. Lots of producer tricks and guest musicians but the energy is somehow lacking.
Blockade (1987)
   Recorded quite well on both A. Tropillo's 8-track and in the 24-track Melodia mobile studio.

Alpha

The Alpha Team (1983)
Races (1984)
Alpha 3 (1985)
Warm Wind (1986)
   The band fronted by Sergei Sarychev, a good singer and formerly keyboard player for Cruise. Hard rock/disco fusion, and a guaranteed smash at provincial dance halls.

Antis

Antis (1986)
   Twelve songs, recorded in Lietuvian TV studios for the video film *Something Has Happened*. The quality is OK but the sound is flat. Antis need to be seen on stage.

Aquarium

The Tales Of Count Diffusor (1977)
All Brothers Are Sisters (1979)
Blue Album (1981)
The Triangle (1981)
Acoustics (1982)
Electricity (1982)
Taboo (1982)
MCI (1983)
Radio Africa (1983)
Day Of The Silver (1984)
December Children (1986)
Ten Arrows (1986)
Equinox (1987)

The first two albums are badly recorded obscure rarities. 'All Brothers' is Bob and Mike's mutual project. 'Acoustics' and 'Electricity' are compilations; side two of the latter is a concert recording from Gruzia 1980, made by Finnish TV. 'MCI' is a Tropillo-made compilation of songs recorded for the 'Taboo' sessions but not included on that album. 'Ten Arrows' is an acoustic concert tape, approved by the band, which features the last recordings of Aquarium's violin player, Alexander Kussul, who later drowned in the Volga.

Aria

Mania Of Grandeur (1985)
Who Are You With (1986)

Professional Moscow heavy metal band with peace loving lyrics and a style similar to Iron Maiden. I can't understand why they're still not on Melodia.

Autograph

Autograph (1984)

The full version of an album which was released by Melodia two years later but cut by half.

Automatic Satisfiers

AY (1985)

All the classic Swine punk songs recorded several years after their initial performance—but this time with tolerable quality.

AVIA

The Life And Works Of Composer Zudov (1985)
Bombay (1986)

One half of the now defunct Strange Games present a clever and paradoxical mixture of ska rhythms, cocktail jazz and quasi-film music, all delivered in extremely ironic fashion.

148

Alexander Bashlachov

The Third Capital (1985)
Time For The Little Bells (1986)
Concert In Taganka Theatre (1986)
Eternal Fast (1987)

Genial and passionate singer/songwriter who committed suicide in February 1988 aged 27. He's never made a fully satisfying studio recording: the ones listed are the best of hundreds of amateur and semi-professional efforts. The second and third last for about two hours and are good quality live recordings. The fourth was recorded on a Yamaha HA cassette 4-track at Sasha Lipnitsky's country cottage and features some of Bashlachov's last works.

Bravo

Bravo (1) (1984)
Bravo (2) (1985)

Both 25-minute mini-albums recorded on 2-track. The first is better, both in quality and performance.

Carnival

Superman (1983)
The Actor (1983)
Radio (1984)
Cabbage (1985)

New wave/pop from Alexander Barykin's band. Later they're transformed into pure easy listening.

Cement

Cement (1985)

The main Russian singing group from Riga. Soviet pop lyrics of the fifties are sung against a musical base of sixties UK rhythm'n'blues.

Centre

Centre (1982)
Stewardess Of The Summer Flights (1983)
A One Room Apartment (1983)
Reading Books In The City Transport (1984)
Thirst For Technics (1984)
The Flower And The Moth (1985)
Signs Of Life (1985)
Learn To Swim (1985)
Favourite Songs (1986)
Rimbaud (1986)
Life Of The Remarkable Men (1986)
My District (1987)
Russians In Their Surroundings (1987)

All albums recorded on 2-track with satisfying quality (except for the very first one). 'Favourite Songs' is the collage of authentic and Centre's versions of Soviet pop hits of the sixties. 'My District' is Vasily Shumov's solo project, recorded by him on synthesizer and computers.

Yuri Chernavsky

Banana Islands (1983)
Automatic Set (1985)

The first LP is perhaps the world's greatest achievement in 2-track recordings. 'Automatic Set' is on 8-track, fully computerised and slightly more boring despite the interesting rhythms and many unusual sounds.

Cloud Area

The Great Harmony (1982)
Secrets Of The Wood (1983)
Artful Self Activity (1983)
The Top Of Cretinism (1984)
A Bastard's Lot (1985)
The Stirrup & The People (1986)

A hard rock band from the northern city of Archangel famous for their angry socially aware lyrics. The recordings were made in Leningrad.

Crematorium

Wine Memories (1984)
Crematorium (1985)
World Of Illusions (1986)
Coma (1988)

Moscow's late answer to Aquarium: folk rock with pretentious lyrics. As there were some objections about the band's name their third album describes them as 'Crem . . .'!

Cruise

Cruise (1982)
The Lifebuoy (1983)
Cruise Around The Planet Of People (1983)
Kikogava (1985)
Rock Forever (1986)
   Valery Gaina, the heavy metal guitar virtuoso, with different sidemen.

DDT

Dust (1982)
Compromise (1983)
The Province (1984)
Time (1986)
Heat In Moscow (1986)
   DDT, and Cloud Area, are the only two bands from distant provinces (here
the city of Ufa, which is beyond the Volga) that became widely popular. Again,
hard rock with some ethnic influences and bitter satirical lyrics. Yuri Shevchuk,
the bandleader and great roaring singer, was forced to leave his native city of
Ufa and now lives and plays in Leningrad. 'Heat In Moscow' is a concert tape
recorded initially by Shevchuk and Sergey Ryzhenko (ex Last Chance, Football
and Time Machine). The only studio album by Football is so awful in quality
that it is not worth hearing.

Dialogue

The Square Man (1982)
Anti-World (1983)
   Good quality modern dance songs. Some of the tracks were later included
on their Melodia album.

DK

I'll Take You To The Tundra (1983)
Little Prince (1984)
Kisiljov (1985)
DMB–85 (1985)
The Hellfire (1986)
   A Moscow underground studio band. From 1983 they've recorded no less
than 33 cassette albums, each with a picture sleeve. These are some of the
more interesting examples. The music varies from kitsch parodies of official
Soviet pop to experimental jazz. Some of their satirical songs are superb but
with such an enormous amount of material, numerous repetitions and simply
unimpressive cuts are inevitable. 'DMB' is authentic modern army folklore with
avant-garde treatment. 'The Hellfire' is DK leader Sergei Zharikov's solo project.

Dr Kinchev & The Style

Nervous Night (1985)

The first, pre-Alisa, recording of Kostia Kinchev, produced with the assistance of his Leningrad friends. Slightly reminiscent of 'Banana Islands'.

Dynamic (The Speaker)

Dynamic (1982)
In Search Of Light (1983)
The Enlightenment (1984)
Answering Machine (1986)
Today And Tomorrow (1987)

The first album is marked by Yuri Chernavsky's inventive arrangements. Generally well played and melodic mainstream rock

Kalinov Bridge

Kalinov Bridge (1987)

The first sparkling of uncompromising rock from Siberia. Sincere performances, poor recording.

Kino

45 (1982)
46 (1983)
The Chairman Of Kamchatka (1984)
This Is Not Love (1985)
The Night (1986)
Blood Group (1988)

The first two albums contain remarkable folk rock, the remainder more straightforward yet melodic rock. '45' was produced by Bob Grebenschikov.

Yuri Loza

Journey To Rock'n'Roll (1983)
The Stars Of Moscow (1984)
Lights Of Stage (1985)
Spleen (1985)

The first cassette was recorded with some help from a group called Primus, the third and fourth with a professional band, The Architects, of whom Loza is now a full-time member. Maybe classified as Soviet pub-rock (although we've got no pubs).

Manufactura

City Affairs (1983)

Nervously sentimental songs performed by the big unfulfilled hope of the Leningrad rock scene.

Yuri Morozov

The Cherry Garden Of Jimi Hendrix (1976)
Wedding Of The Cretins (1978)
The Wanderings Of A Blue Star (1981)
Auto Da Fe (1985)

This man has recorded about 60 cassettes in more than 10 years. These are the most popular. As is clear from the titles, this is progressive rock seventies style.

Muhomor (Fly-Agaric)

Golden Album (1983)

Recorded with no musical instruments at all. This is a collage of classical, pop and rock recordings, absurdist poems and sketches made by a group of Moscow conceptualist painters. In some parts it's very funny and undoubtedly quite ahead of its time. Some of those involved now participate in Central Russian Height.

The Myths

Second Beginning (1980)
The Homebound Road (1982)

An average Leningrad blues rock band. Unfortunately there are no recordings of The Myths in the seventies when Yuri Llechenko was the band's leader.

Nastya

Tatsu (1987)

Nastya Poleva, ex-Trek girl singer, has made this nice tape with the help of every top rock musician from Sverdlovsk.

Nautilus

At The Italian Opera (1985)
I Am Invincible (1985)
The Parting (1986)

A stylish and lyrically quite provocative new wave band from Sverdlovsk. Each album is better than its predecessor, so Nautilus are probably the best Russian band outside of Moscow and Leningrad.

New Composers

The Cosmic Space (1983)
Wind Of Changes (1984)
Perception Of Verbalisation (1985)

Igor Verichev and Valery Alahov from Leningrad work with synthesizers, tapes and loop effects, mixing some Eno-like ambient music with scratch reworkings of Soviet TV and radio programmes. In the pipeline is a new tape album dedicated to Yuri Gagarin.

Nicolai Copernicus

Motherland (1986)

Monotonous psychedelic new wave music which reminds me of David Sylvian or The Cure. Recorded on 4-track.

Night Avenue

Unfamiliar Faces (1984)
Microbes Of Love (1985)
Colours Of The Golden Years (1986)
Humanitarian Life (1986)
Democracy And Discipline (1987)

Night Avenue started off by imitating Soft Cell, then flirted with electronic rockabilly and, more recently, began to sound more experimental and not unlike early Cabaret Voltaire. Singer/guitarist Alexey Borisov has also made one commercial tape called 'Richness' (1985), while keyboard player Ivan Sokolovsky has made two avant-garde cassettes—'Works Of Different Years' (1986) and 'TVD—Gugenlohe' (1987). On 'Humanitarian Life' two songs are sung by Zhanna Aguzarova from Bravo.

The Object Of Mockery

Greedy Things (1986)
Glasnost (1987)

A cross between mainstream rock and punk, this band is led by a guy nicknamed Ricochet and they made their debut at Leningrad's Rock Club festival of 1986.

Picnic

The Smoke (1982)
Wolf Dance (1984)
Hieroglyph (1986)

This group began with hard rock and 'problem' lyrics but now play computer orientated new wave and work for Philharmonia. An inoffensive Leningrad band who never made it really big, probably because of a lack of identity and fresh ideas.

Polite Refusal

Opera 86 (1986)

One of the best bands from the Moscow Rock Lab, eclectic style from reggae to blues and 'noise' music. Interesting futuristic lyrics.

Rossiyanye

Rossiyanye (1984)

A compilation of tracks of various origins, this was released some time after the mysterious disappearance of Georgy Ordanovsky, the group's leader. This is the only material documentation of this wild Leningrad band.

Secret

Alice (1983)

Non-Stop (1986)

Mersey sounds from the banks of the Neva. 'Alice' is extremely amateurish, both in recording and performance. 'Non-Stop' is the prototype for the first Melodia LP.

Sonans

Sonans (1978)

Chaugrin Skin (1980)

The first tape is instrumental Prokofiev influenced compositions for a rock band with string section. The second is Alexander Pantykin's attempt at straight rock but is still very strange with a dominant ostinato piano sound. Both works were sadly underrated at the time, mainly because Sverdlovsk is too far away from the main rock centres.

Stereo-Zoldat

Asphalt (1986)

Minimalistic avant-garde rock mockery from Leningrad. Lead vocalist Anton Odosinsky now appears live with AVIA.

Strange Games

Metamorphoses (1983)

Watch Out (1985)

The best (and virtually the only) Soviet ska band. Tracks from both these tapes are featured on the American 'Red Wave' album.

Sunday

Sunday (1981)

Who Is To Blame (1983)

Moscow Time (1984)

Popular group in the Time Machine tradition.

Tambourine

The Bug On The Comb (1985)

Arty folk-rock: some excellent melodies and sophisticated arrangements. Tambourine's front man, Vladimir Levy, has also made a solo tape—'The Little Wheel' (1983).

Televisor

Televisor (1985)

Still the only studio tape from Mikhail Borzykin's group, recorded on 8-track by A. Tropillo. 'Get Out Of Control' and other 'glasnost-era' tours-de-force from this hot Leningrad band exist only as live bootlegs.

The Bugle Call

The Bugle Call (1982)

   Bible-inspired pomp rock. There is an English language version of this tape in existence.

Time Machine

Time Machine (1978)
The Sunny Island (1979)
Songs 80–82 (1982)
Aliens Among Aliens (1984)
Fish In A Can (1985)

   The first three tapes were recorded at the Moscow Theatre College and various TV studios. 'Fish In A Can' is a mini-album, the last before the group's collaboration with Melodia, and part of it is included in their first official LP. Andrey Makarevich also made two acoustic solo cassettes in 1983 and 1985.

Trek

Trek (1981)
Who Are You (1982)
Trek III (1983)

   Sonans, without Pantykin, attempting to repeat the success of 'Chaugrin Skin' but sounding only monotonous. The group disbanded after the third cassette album.

Urfin Juice

The Journey (1981)
15 (1982)
Heavy Metal Lifestyle (1984)

   Disappointed with the avant-garde, A. Pantykin turned to heavy rock but the results weren't very impressive. More interesting is his solo project with some ex-Sonans friends, 'The Cabinet' (1986). UJ's guitarist, one Yegor Belkin, has made a solo tape, 'About Radio' (1985).

Vova Sinij

Astudia (1984)
Blue Bulbs Play (1985)
Shut Up! (1985)
Hally-Gally (1986)
Can't Keep From Singing (1986)

   Tape loop masters from Chelyabinsk. The rhythm tracks are borrowed from a wide range of Western acts from Donna Summer to Talking Heads. The recent albums, besides additional vocals, also feature some sax, guitar and synthesizers. Great conception, funny lyrics. The band's name is different on each album: from 'Vova Sinij & The Brothers In Mind' to 'A Certain S'.

Visokosnoye Leto (Leap Year Summer)

Prometheus (1979)

A double play tape from the founding fathers of Soviet art rock includes the rock opera 'Prometheus Enchained' and further laconic compositions.

Yellow Postmen

Bolderay Railroad (1981)
We Love The New Wave (1982)
Alice (1984)
Always Quietly (1984)
Depressive City (1987)

Strangely sounding electronic pop with some very bleak yet captivating melody lines. Ingus Baushkenieks, the singer, bass player and producer, has also released a solo tape recorded purely from a Casio CZ 101 which is very good quality for a 2-track recording.

Zoo

Blues De Moscou (1982)
Smalltown N (1983)
White Line (1984)

Lively and dirty r'n'b with juicy lyrics, all recorded on 2-track. The first cassette is live in Moscow. A new album entitled 'Illusions' is due very soon. There are also two solo tapes by Mike Naumenko, 'Sweet N And Others' (1980) and 'LV' (1982). The first is mainly two guitars and vocals, the second incorporates a rhythm box and instrumental contributions from assorted members of Aquarium and Zoo.

Zvuki Mu

Live In Moscow, Rock Festival 1986 (1986)

As all attempts at studio recordings by Zvuki Mu have collapsed, this is the best and most popular of their live tapes, although it's not recognised by the band as their debut cassette. Recorded at the Rock Lab Festival in June 1986, it includes 'The Soviet Press' and other big hits.

APPENDIX III

SELECTED FILMOGRAPHY

Full-length movies

The Soul (1981)
A musical melodrama with Time Machine as the backing band, some Soviet pop stars and some Makarevich songs.

Start From Scratch (1986)
Starring Andrey Makarevich as a struggling bard working by day as a janitor.

The Hat (1982)
A musical comedy, strangely featuring the very serious Autograph.

Hit Song Of That Summer (1985)
Melodramatic pop music, including performances by some Estonian rock bands including Rock Hotel, Vitamin, Ruya and Apelsin. One can even spot the face of Peter Volkonsky and Hardy Volmer in some scenes.

The Place We Are Not In (1986)
Teenage comedy starring Gunnar Graps and his Magnetic Band.

Four White Shirts (1970)
A film about early Lietuvian hippies and rockers, with the participation of Imant Kalninsh and Double Ladybug. It wasn't recommended for showing in cinemas but can occasionally be seen in small clubs in Riga.

The Burglar (1987)
A detective story about juvenile delinquents and rock musicians. Kostia Kinchev plays one of the main roles while Alisa, Auction and AVIA all perform songs.

Assa (1987)
Love triangle melodrama starring Sergey Bugaev of Popular Mechanics and Victor Tsoy. Featuring live appearances by Kino and tracks from Aquarium, Bravo and Yuri Chernavsky. Funny in parts but generally disappointing considering the hype that attended its release.

Short Movies (Diploma works of cinema students.)

Ivanov (1983, 10 minutes)
Boris Grebenschikov alone, plus one minute of Aquarium.

End Of Holidays (1986, 30 minutes)
Presents Victor Tsoy and Kino in Kiev.

Yahha (1987, 40 minutes)
Shows the life and style of Leningrad's alternative youth and includes appearances by Alisa, Kino and Zoo. Recommended.

Rok (1988, 90 minutes)
Portrays five heroes of Leningrad rock—Boris Grebenschikov, Victor Tsoy, Anton of AVIA, Spitball of Auction and Yuri Schevchuk of DDT—not only at concerts but also at home and at 'day-time' work. This is a unique film, quite essential in order to understand Soviet rock lifestyles and background.

Documentaries

Is It Easy To Be Young? (1986, 80 minutes)
Includes several minutes of the Lietuvian hard rock band Perkuns, but generally a true picture of various 'problem youth' communities. A quite amazing and very famous 'glasnost' attempt.

Six Letters About Beat, (1977, 20 minutes)
Presents the Moscow rock scene of the mid-seventies: Time Machine, Leap Year Summer and Ruby Attack.

Musical Mirror (1984, 30 minutes)
Directed by Janus Nygisto, Ruya's guitar player, and presenting—besides his own band—Rock Hotel and In Spe.

Videofilms

Something Happened (1986, 60 minutes)
An Antis extravaganza, also featuring other Lietuvian rock bands including Vitas Kemagis' group and Foyer.